Interior MOTIVES

DESIGNING A CAREER WITH PASSION

—DEBBE DALEY—

Advantage | Books

Published by Advantage, Charleston, South Carolina.
Member of Advantage Media.

ADVANTAGE is a registered trademark, and the Advantage colophon is a trademark of Advantage Media Group, Inc.

Printed in the United States of America.

10 9 8 7 6 5 4 3 2 1

ISBN: 978-1-64225-392-4 (Paperback)
ISBN: 978-1-64225-648-2 (eBook)

LCCN: 2022918555

Cover design by Analisa Smith.
Layout design by Megan Elger.

This publication is designed to provide accurate and authoritative information in regard to the subject matter covered. It is sold with the understanding that the publisher is not engaged in rendering legal, accounting, or other professional services. If legal advice or other expert assistance is required, the services of a competent professional person should be sought.

Advantage Media helps busy entrepreneurs, CEOs, and leaders write and publish a book to grow their business and become the authority in their field. Advantage authors comprise an exclusive community of industry professionals, idea-makers, and thought leaders. Do you have a book idea or manuscript for consideration? We would love to hear from you at **AdvantageMedia.com**.

Contents

DEDICATION

TO MY DAUGHTER, KRISTA: you have been my sole motivation and driving force to create a life of passion without hesitation. Watching you adapt to all life throws our way makes us even stronger. The ups and downs have been a lot, and the path was worth the journey. We've learned together how to overcome. Together forever. I love you.

TO MY PARENTS: Thank you, Dad, for your constant strength and guidance and for always being the rock in our family, especially when we are at our worst. You have taught me how to be genuine in everything life brings and, most of all, integrity.

Mom, watching you care for your family and welcome others into ours without judgement has always been inspiring. You have created a haven to which your children are never afraid to come home. Your every detail, manners, etiquette, thoughtfulness, and love for your children has inspired me to do the same.

Thank you both for creating a happy home life to grow from, and a heritage of old-world upbringing to be proud of. I love you.

TO MY GRANDPARENTS: You will never have the opportunity to read this book and will never know the impact your lives have had on my being as a creative and the person I am today—one who looks at life and sees all the simple pleasures. I love you in heaven.

TO MY HUSBAND, JAMIE: Thank you for always being by my side. You are my rock. Your ability and insight to read every situation is your gift. Thank you for letting me be my stubborn self, until I come to you for your advice. Your business sense has guided and pushed me to levels I would normally hesitate to achieve. Let the adventures continue. As our priest said at our wedding, "We saved the best for last." I love you.

ACKNOWLEDGMENTS

The creation of this book has been made possible with the help of the Advantage|Forbes Books team. Their professionalism, stringent schedule, follow-up, and planning has not gone without notice. After years of trying to share my story with a purpose of inspiring others to follow their passion, shed the negativity, and go for their dream career, *Interior Motives: Designing a Career with Passion* has been made a reality.

My sincere thank-you to Jennifer Holt, for her enthusiastic listening skills and assistance in bringing this content to life in my words, in my story. I am so grateful to have worked with her as my writing partner on this journey.

I would like to thank Ann Anderson for showing me how to share my own creativity and open up the doors for opportunity with my business. Showing how to put myself out there, to ask for what I want and not to sit and wait for things to happen, was a true lesson learned. Ann has been such an inspiration while teaching me how to diversify my business and pushing me to go to the next level. For this, I am forever grateful. *Thank you.*

INTRODUCTION

*S*ometimes the little things that hold our attention—
the things we always find ourselves gravitating
toward—can have the biggest effects on who we
become over the course of a lifetime.

The person who I am today, for example, turns out to have been
strongly influenced by the joy I took in playing house as a child.

My interest in playing house was like that of many other children
my age, but there was something about the intensity with which I
approached each detail and the pleasure I took in all the hours devoted
to imagining and creating those details that made them have a lasting
influence on the things I've come to enjoy as an adult.

As a child, I took every opportunity I could to make things,
whether it was mud pies in the enamel-coated metal bowl that was
always sitting out in our garden or the treehouse that my brother and
I built from wood scraps. And I treated my Betty Crocker Easy-Bake
Oven like it was a true chef's tool—making cakes from the simple
to the more elaborate. Every Greek household had two kitchens—
because how can you cook all that food during the holidays in just one
oven?—so I'd be in the downstairs kitchen cooking with my Easy-Bake
Oven and then setting a table of white-and-blue Pfaltzgraff-patterned

plastic dishes for my dolls while my mother would be cooking and setting the table for our family dinner upstairs.

She would call down to me, "Debbe, dinner is ready."

"Okay! I'll be right up as soon as I'm done making dinner here," I'd call back.

The house that built me—my childhood home in Dracut, Massachusetts.

The ceiling orbs behind me in this picture (left) now hang in our own home (right).

Later, when I was twelve years old, my grandparents gifted me my first sewing machine—a Singer—that they'd picked up at a yard sale. My maternal grandmother (who'd died when she was just forty) had been a seamstress, and my step-grandmother and my mother were also sewers. I'd inherited some of my grandmother's belongings, including her books on woodworking and her fashion sketches— which I treasured. From the sketches and family stories, I understood that she was quite the seamstress, making beautiful party and holiday dresses for my mother and her sisters when the family could not afford to purchase such finery from the shops.

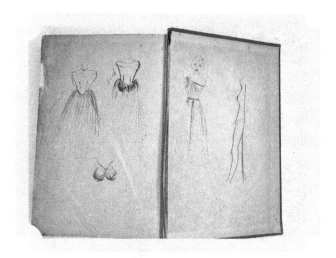

My grandmother's dress sketches.

My Grandmother Bessie Delazanos in her handmade coat, 1947.

My first quilt made with my grandmother and my mother.

My mother saved all her fabric scraps, and I used those to play with different stitches and figure out the method to the madness of creating clothing and crafts. I would try my hand at making dresses with no pattern and was always helping my mother and step-grandmother sew blankets until the time when I could make my own.

My mother had organized colorful spools of thread in one of the cabinet drawers, and in another, she had acquired quite a collection of buttons—all shapes and sizes, and in materials from plastic and cloth to wood and metal. I would play for hours with my new sewing machine, treating the drawers of threads and buttons as my own private notions section of a five-and-dime store.

As a child of Greek immigrants, I didn't just have access to traditional linens and the antique furnishings both my grandfathers had acquired; I also learned the stories that were embedded in those materials. I came to appreciate old and valuable things, whether they were picked up at yard sales or passed along from family to family, generation to generation.

My father had come to America with his father and his four siblings when he was just nine years old. My paternal grandmother had also passed away at an early age, and my grandfather was left with five young children, one of whom—my uncle—was just two years old at the time. My grandfather's sister and brother had already emigrated to the US when he made the decision to bring his children to America and start a new life.

My Grandfather Nicholas Cakounes with his five children coming to America.

After they made the journey through Ellis Island, the boys were sent to Dracut, Massachusetts, to live and work with my grandfather's sister on her family's farm. The girls were sent to Belmont, Massachusetts, to live with my grandfather's brother and his family. When my grandfather had saved up enough money, he bought a farmhouse in Dracut and brought the children back together there.

My parents were introduced to one another through what I'll call the big Greek family network in the region. My father delivered eggs for the Vrouhas chicken farm in Chelmsford, Massachusetts, at the same time that my aunt Cookie was dating the chicken farmer's son, Spiro. My mother's parents were friends of Spiro's parents, so the two families were already well acquainted. Aunt Cookie introduced my mother to my father, and our family grew from there. The Vrouhas farm became a gathering place for our families and others to celebrate Greek Orthodox Easter.

From left to right: my sister Kathy, brother Nick, my mom, and me at the Greek Easter at the Vrouhas Farm.

Greek Orthodox Easter at the Vrouhas Farm.

By the time my brother and I were young children, it had become a regular event on Sundays to visit my maternal grandparents in Nashua, New Hampshire. We'd have Sunday dinner with my grandfather, Papou Delazanos, and step-grandmother, YiaYia Georgia, and then travel back to Dracut to have dessert with my paternal grandfather, Papou Cakounes. Papou Cakounes would always have leftover chicken that he had cooked in a cast-iron skillet on his big old black cast-iron stove, and he would leave it out for us to pick at. For dessert, he would make a frosted chocolate cake from scratch—little unmixed balls of flour visible in each slice.

It was at Papou Cakounes's old farmhouse that my obsession with home furnishings developed.

Like for most of us, there's a lot I don't remember about my childhood, and then there are some things that stand out vividly in all their detail. That's what Papou Cakounes's whole house was like for me. I remember walking up the front stairs and into the little hallway with its mahogany banister and newel post. The parlor was off to the left of the front entrance and had a formal camelback-style sofa and loveseat upholstered in an emerald-gold velvet. There was also a wingback chair with the same camelback frame and an old phonograph standing next to it. The mantel had black-and-white pictures of my father and his siblings spread across its entirety. There were oriental rugs in that room as well as in the dining room and main hallway.

Papou Cakounes with my Aunt Genie on the front steps of the farmhouse.

An old newel post.

Pocket doors separated the living and dining rooms. A tall empire-style dresser in the dining room displayed a vintage lemonade set—white milk glass with pastel stripes of red, green, yellow, and orange—each glass held in a stand, with an ice bucket of the same design featured in the middle. The dining room had a pantry closet with a brown marble door handle, and the shelves inside were filled with all kinds of cookies and snacks. Getting into the pantry and breaking into the vanilla wafers and chocolate-covered marshmallow cookies was one of my brother's and my favorite things to do when we visited—bested only by picking pears, strawberries, and mulberries outside in the summertime.

There were twin-sized beds with pillows strewn about them in both the dining room and the kitchen. As a child, I never understood their purpose—they simply contributed to the overall aura of the house for me, just one more point of curiosity among many. Since then, I've come to understand them as part of my Greek heritage, reflecting the importance of daytime siestas. But at that time, the presence of a resting place in the kitchen remained an oddity. The rest of the kitchen, however, was the most amazing place: it was the life-size version of my imaginary Betty Crocker kitchen at home.

Not far from the daybed was a black table with a porcelain white top. The table had a pullout drawer for keeping silverware, and the tabletop had a rooster design that reminded me of the Kellogg's Corn Flakes cereal box. The sink cabinet was made of beadboard—to match the bottoms of the walls—and held a one-piece porcelain sink with a grooved countertop that drained into it. The faucet was mounted off the wall on a marble backsplash slab, which contrasted beautifully with the old black cast-iron cooking stove.

I got to know every nook and cranny of that farmhouse interior. I've carried all those details with me, to the surprise of the rest of my family members. To this day, I'll remember something about a particular design feature or piece of furniture, and no one else in my family will have the vaguest clue what I'm talking about.

Given these experiences from my formative years, you might think I have a straightforward story to tell about my career, something like this: I loved homemaking and home furnishings from a very early age and turned that into a successful lifelong career in interior design from the moment I left my parents' house and set out on my own.

That is not the story I have to tell.

Those influences and interests from my childhood took a back seat for quite some time, and it wasn't until I was faced with different challenges in my adult life that I came to understand—and chose to act on—the things I most loved to spend my time doing.

I'm going to tell you more of that story in this book, because I've come to believe that at least two things are extremely important when we talk about shaping the trajectories of our lives, about consciously choosing what we do for work and for fun rather than just doing whatever happens to come our way.

It wasn't until I was faced with different challenges in my adult life that I came to understand—and chose to act on—the things I most loved to spend my time doing.

The first is this: *it is possible to turn the little things we genuinely love to do into a source of income.* I'm not going to tell you that it's easy, but I absolutely do believe that it is possible to monetize your passions. I'll tell you about how I did just that and how I've been helping others do the same.

The second is that *sometimes we have to step back and try to find, or remember, what it is that we enjoy, what motivates us creatively.* Figuring that out can involve some soul-searching work. It usually also requires us to have the courage to think of ourselves as works in progress, to acknowledge and address our own doubts and fears, and to face down any naysayers who want to critique our choices or point out all the obstacles to our success.

My husband and I always talk about the work we do decorating and taking care of our home as "our art project." Our house is a work in progress. There's a lot of trying out and playing around with color, light, furnishings—and the scene is ever evolving. Over the years, I've also come to think about life as being engaged in an art project. You start out with an idea and some inspiration and try to keep an eye on where you think you might be headed, knowing full well that the project is sure to shift and change as you go, that you'll always be making changes to your canvas. That very idea is what motivates me to share with you how I clarified (and continue to clarify) my own vision for my life and how I found (and continue to find) ways to turn creative activities that I enjoy into a steady source of income.

Let me be clear: this isn't a book about getting rich from doing what you love. Instead, it's a book about figuring out how you can spend more of your time discovering and then actually doing what interests you. More than that, this is a book about approaching your life creatively by keeping your interests alive rather than pushing them aside or—worse—actively giving up on them.

Think about life as being engaged in an art project ... knowing full well that the project is sure to shift and change as you go, that you'll always be making changes to your canvas.

If that sounds good to you, read on! If you're not sure you believe me that it can be done, *please* read on! I want to convince and empower you to do more—a lot more—of what you love.

Chapter One

WHAT DRIVES YOUR CREATIVITY?

*I*n the seventh grade, a woman came to talk to our class about what we were going to do when we grew up. The movie *9 to 5* had just come out in theaters—with Lily Tomlin, Dolly Parton, and Jane Fonda all playing working women in the corporate world—and it had quickly become a reflection of women's ambitions at that time: women were stepping out of their homes and into the corporate scene to pursue "real careers"—many of them as secretaries.

Back during that classroom presentation, and even later, once it was time for me to apply to college, I didn't know that interior design was a career option, let alone one that I could have studied and prepared for with a specialized degree. Much later, it would also become clear to me that "what we want to be when we grow up" and what appeals to us career-wise is often less a reflection of what we wish for or enjoy and more about what we're exposed to—both what's offered to us and what we see (or don't see) other people around us doing with their lives.

My plan was to attend Fisher College, a business school on Newberry Street in Boston. More than anything, I wanted to be independent and move away from my strict Greek family home, so I regularly brought brochures to my father that highlighted all of Fisher's amenities and educational benefits.

What appeals to us career-wise is often less a reflection of what we wish for or enjoy and more about what we're exposed to.

Dad would not have any of it, especially the part about me living away from home. So, I ended up attending an all-girls business school run by the Sisters of Mercy called Castle Junior College, located in Windham, New Hampshire. Castle was a thirty-minute drive from my house, and to get there each day, I drove the family 1970s Lincoln Continental, a true boat of a vehicle, through the winding back roads and hills of New Hampshire.

Castle was a professional college that graduated young women into careers in business. The college dress code required that we wear to class what we would be expected to wear to the office jobs we were preparing to take on—in the 1980s, that amounted to a suit coat and a skirt. I enjoyed my time at Castle, and as the school promised, I graduated with an associate's degree and a job. I was hired as the executive secretary for the stockbroker who started the Lowell, Massachusetts, office of the firm Kidder Peabody.

To claim my independence from my strict family and finally live outside the house, I chose to marry my high school sweetheart. My father was none too pleased about that. He didn't like my high school sweetheart and barely talked to me for six months after I got engaged. On my wedding day, he held both my hands before walking me down the aisle, tears in his eyes, and said, "We can go home now. We don't have to do this." I knew there were some red flags—my high school sweetheart's possessiveness, his jealousy—but I loved the idea of freedom that marriage offered, and I was eager to make a home in the ways I'd imagined and played at as a kid.

I sewed all the window treatments for our first house, and when my mother saw them, she asked me to make some for her house too. I also loved going to the office every day. In a way, my appreciation for the corporate world was tied to my sense of independence from the family house. I made new friends. I learned about the stock market, and I even got to place orders for affluent clients. After just one year at Kidder Peabody, I decided that I wanted to become a stockbroker. When I approached the office manager with the idea of having the firm sponsor my preparation, he laughed out loud and let me know in no uncertain terms that this industry really was *not* for women.

But I am a Cakounes girl, which is to say that I have inherited a certain stubbornness. When someone tells me that I cannot do something ... well, those are basically fighting words. When the office manager dismissed my interest, I didn't feel driven to become a stockbroker at some other firm, but I did feel driven to succeed in the corporate world, generally speaking. That very afternoon, I started my search for a new job—and landed in the finance department of a newspaper printer manufacturing company.

I was good at what I did, so I quickly moved up the ladder at that company and eventually moved over into human resources. Our boss treated us well—so well, in fact, that the company went bankrupt from his overspending. In the end, it was my job to serve all the employees their pink slips—a demoralizing and confidence-shattering task. Afterward, I decided I would take the summer off *to figure out what I really wanted to do.*

I was twenty-two years old and unsure about my career path, but I was also driven, and I didn't much like being unproductive. My way of "figuring out" what to do was to apply for a temporary position with Wang Laboratories—a computer hardware company. The Wang towers were in Lowell, and my job was up on the tenth floor, once again in the finance department.

The temporary position eventually turned into a permanent one. This time, though, I knew that the job I had taken was not really what I wanted. I'd started to notice a difference between what I was good at doing and what I actually wanted to spend my time doing, between what *looked* like a good thing to do and what *felt* good to do. So far, I'd done good work at each job I had taken. But I also didn't necessarily *want* those jobs.

Quite frankly, I'd started to feel similarly about my marriage. I was frustrated by the fact that my husband was envious that I earned more money at my corporate jobs than he did as a grocery store department manager. I was frustrated by his need to show off the material things we had accumulated in the short while we'd been married, and I was frustrated that he did not appreciate the close relationship I continued to have with my family.

I continued in my position at Wang but decided to go back to school for interior design and applied to the night program at Middlesex Community College in Bedford, Massachusetts. That was the first of several changes in my career that did not give me a sense of moving forward in any meaningful way. Instead, it felt like I was turning back. Even in my early twenties, there was something scary about putting time, energy, and money into getting that new degree. I felt unsure about my goals, and I sensed that my curiosity about shifting away from a career climbing the ladder in a corporate environment was distressing to the people around me—especially my father, who wanted nothing more than for his children to hold jobs that offered economic security.

Earlier, I pointed out that many of us are directed toward a limited set of job options. I'd add that we are mostly encouraged not to doubt whether any of those options will make us feel fulfilled. I am thankful that my stubbornness helped me stand strong against my own doubts about trying to switch over into a career in interior design. When I signed up for those night classes, I felt like I was taking a chance on something I really enjoyed, even though I couldn't foresee whether there would be any payoff career-wise. Looking back on it now, I associate my willingness to try something new with that growing sense of deep frustration. I see, too, how that wouldn't be the first time frustration with my circumstances would compel me to make some dramatic changes.

Between the window treatments I'd sewn for our house and the ones I'd made for my parents' house, I started getting word-of-mouth referrals and requests. People would bring me fabric, and I'd talk with them about what they wanted, design the window treatments with them, then sew. We built out a workroom in the downstairs of our house, and I even started giving sewing classes on the side—mostly just for friends. To facilitate the sewing, I found part-time employment doing sales work for Matrix Technologies. I coordinated trade shows and provided administrative support for the president and vice president of the company. I also worked with Premier Fastener, as a salesperson, selling fasteners for commercial boilers—the sort you'd find in hospitals, manufacturing environments, really any operation with a smokestack. To get started, I had to buy a specific drill, then attend a week-long training during which I learned about bits and fasteners, titanium and stainless steel, and practiced giving demonstrations of our products. I worked at Matrix, sewed window treatments in the evenings and on weekends, got pregnant and gave birth to our daughter, Krista, and felt the happiest I had in some time.

The first pair of custom drapes made for my parents' home in the early '80s.

That changed when my husband hurt his back at work and decided to take a settlement offer. That in itself wouldn't necessarily have been an issue, but he also decided that we should sell our house in Massachusetts and build a new house and a new life in Florida. While our new home was being built, the three of us moved in with my parents for six months. That was a very stressful, very anxiety-filled period. I took solace in the time I spent with Krista as well as the time I spent making window treatments and placing furniture orders for the Florida house.

But by the time we were ready to move away, I'd come to believe that going with my husband to Florida and setting up our new home there amounted to nothing less than a final attempt on my part to save a dying marriage.

Nowadays, when I talk about creativity, I tend to make a distinction between being driven to succeed, generally speaking, and being tuned in to what drives one's creativity, specifically. When I started out in the corporate world, I thought that achieving success there was exactly what I wanted. I discovered that I could do well the jobs that were offered to me, and I took some satisfaction in my achievements. But my creativity was not tapped or activated by those jobs. And for all the feeling of moving forward with my life—moving out of my parents' house, getting married and starting a family, climbing the corporate ladder—I still hadn't answered the question at the heart of tuning into our creative impulses, the question *What is going to make me happy?*

As a young person, I wasn't yet able to recognize what mattered to me most and what would genuinely make me happy. I think that's true for a lot of us when we're young. Although I had managed to turn back and embrace my childhood love of sewing, I also hadn't come to see taking those design courses or making window treatments as in any way central to building the life I wanted. At best, I imagined sewing treatments as a side project, a way to bring in a little extra money while I worked at a job that offered me a steady income, insurance and retirement benefits, and the security of ongoing employment.

That's why I would encourage anyone who is unsure about what interests and drives them creatively to take a look back. On the one hand, that means looking all the way back to the things you liked to do as a child or young person at play. What were the activities that gave you pleasure? Have you carried them with you through your life? If so, in what ways? If not, why not? On the other hand, taking a look back means looking "back" at the ways you play as an adult—to your hobbies and interests and the way you feel when you're engaged with them. What activities bring you pleasure now? Which of those things do you feel a strong need to keep doing? Which do you imagine carrying forward to make a happy future for yourself? In both instances, you're identifying your foundation—and that can be both scary and invigorating at once.

It's important to remember one's interests and passions, because we can so easily get distracted from them, or look for them in all the wrong directions, or even learn to believe that they're not worthwhile. Being good at things we don't love doing can itself distract us from identifying or remembering what we genuinely love and want to do. Learning to separate all that noise from what really makes you happy is an important first step toward knowing and naming your passions and then figuring out how to make sure those passions are being fed by what you do to earn a living.

You can earn money doing anything. The idea I encourage you to take seriously is that you can also earn money doing something you absolutely love to do.

Honestly, you can earn money doing anything. The idea I encourage you to take seriously is that you can also earn money *doing something you absolutely love to do.* The point is not the money making; the point is being happy with what you are doing with your time and where you are putting your energy. When I eventually understood what drove me creatively, my goal was straightforward: to pursue my happy life and still be able to pay the bills.

Chapter Two

FIND YOUR PATH,
AND GET ON IT

I sewed custom treatments for every window in the big house we built in Florida. When we finally arrived there, my husband was in a hurry to get the entire place decorated; he wanted to take pictures and send them back home as a way of bragging to family and friends. We'd moved some furniture into storage before leaving Massachusetts, and I worked hard during our first month in Florida to ensure that all of it was reupholstered to fit with the furnishings we'd recently acquired. It took about three months for us to set up the house and for my husband to find work. When everything felt settled, I was more convinced than ever that moving to a new house in a faraway state wasn't going to resolve any of my frustrations with our marriage.

We didn't agree on things that mattered. I found my husband lacking in compassion—even when it came to his own family members—but also smothering at the same time; there was a lot of unhappiness and a lot of arguing between us. I'd started to see that while it would be one thing for me to choose to stay with him, it was another thing entirely to choose to raise Krista around him. About the time that she started worrying aloud whether her mommy and daddy loved her, I decided it would be a healthy decision to get a divorce.

There was too much negativity in our relationship, and I didn't want Krista growing up around that any longer. I also didn't care what anyone was going to think—not even my family—if I left our marriage to become a single mom back in Massachusetts. I'd been thinking of leaving for the last two of the seven years we'd been married. In my mind, I was ready to move forward as an independent single mother.

I had a plan to return to Dracut for my ten-year high school reunion, but my husband's new job prevented him from making the trip along with me. In light of that fact, I arranged a two-week visit home for Krista and me. I needed to have some difficult conversations with family and see about finding my way there on my own. How would I support us when we moved back to Dracut? Where would we live?

While I was visiting family and friends, my husband was tracking my every move. "Why didn't you stay with my parents on Tuesday?" he'd ask. "Just who were you with last night when you went out for dinner?" He called everyone he knew to find out exactly where I was or what time I got in at night. His questions were endless, and his tendency to suspiciousness and jealousy was at an all-time high.

Back when I'd left my part-time job at Matrix Technologies so that we could move to Florida, my future sister-in-law, who was the office manager at Matrix, handed me a sweet note that promised, "When you come back, you will have a job full time waiting for you here." During my visit home, she scheduled me a meeting with the company president, who already knew me from my part-time work there and who offered me a job as his direct assistant.

When it came to telling my parents that I did not want to be married anymore, I started with my mother. We were driving to check out the new mall in town when I raised the subject. She turned to me and said, "Well, you know, you're going to have to tell your father."

I knew.

Ours was a family with no divorces, strongly committed to pre-serving tradition and heritage.

Later that afternoon, the three of us were in the kitchen together, my mother preparing dinner, then looking over at me suggestively, then turning back to the stove, then looking over at me again. I was nervous, but my father was kind. He hugged me and said, "I will be by your side no matter what you decide to do. Whatever you need, we will be here for you."

My youngest sister, Gina, who was thirteen years old at the time, and Krista, who was three, both traveled back to Florida with me. Gina had been scheduled to make the return trip with us, and my parents had planned to meet up with us a week later for a visit to the new house. So, it wasn't the most unusual thing when I returned to Florida with my sister.

My husband had planned an apologetic welcome. He'd bought me flowers and gifts and had transformed the bedroom into a romantic oasis.

I could hear Gina and Krista playing out by the pool when I took as deep a breath as I could muster and accessed my resolve: "The house is set up. You've gotten a job, and that's great, but I don't want to be married anymore. I'm going home."

He was enraged. "Did you cheat on me? Who did you see while you were in Dracut?"

"This has been coming for a long …" He shoved me onto the bed and tried to rip the wedding ring off my finger.

When I wriggled out of his grasp and stood up, he lunged forward and hit me, then chased me as I ran toward the bathroom.

My little sister heard the screaming from the yard. She and Krista ran to my husband's cousin's house across the street to call for the police. The result of all the commotion was that my husband was required to leave the house for the night.

Still panicked after he'd left the house, I called my parents back home in Dracut. My mother contacted the family lawyer, and the first thing he said when he called me was "You'd better check your bank account." When I arrived at the bank the next morning, true to expectation, my husband had withdrawn all our money.

My parents flew down immediately.

My father purchased airline tickets for me and Krista and paid to have my car transported back to Dracut. Within a few days, my husband and I were talking about selling the house, something my husband really didn't want to do. Neither did his mother, who had been looking forward to showing it off to all her friends.

Of all the furnishings in the Florida house, all I wanted to take home with me was Krista's bedroom set and the sewing machine that my grandfather and step-grandmother had gifted me with when I was young. I wanted the former so that Krista would have some sense of continuity and safety during the upheaval, and I wanted the latter to keep hold of that gift that had meant so much to me as a child. I remembered a conversation I'd had not a week earlier with the president of Matrix Technologies. He'd taken me out to lunch as part of my interview to become his secretary, and over salads, he'd said, "You'll have your daughter, and that's all you need to start over. Everything else can be replaced." He was exactly right.

I needed my child and my family, my sewing machine, and not much of anything else.

I was convinced that I was taking a big step to change my and Krista's lives for the better. Starting over didn't have to be a setback. Starting over could also mean moving in the direction of all the positive things that could happen for the two of us.

Krista and I lived with my parents for six months while I took up my new position at Matrix and searched for a more permanent place for us to call home. When I first started looking, I had my eye on a dilapidated old cottage that I was excited to fix up. I would drag my father and my brother with me to check out all these old fixer-uppers. They both responded with the same refrain: "Deb, who is going to do all the work on these places? You will be working all day and then go home as a single mom to a place that's way out in the woods." My father thought it safer to find a condo close to my parents and let them help out with Krista. The condo I finally selected—having agreed that it was the far more sensible choice at that moment in our lives—had an attached garage and a large, fenced yard for Krista to play in.

My husband decided to go through with selling the Florida house. The money from that sale would help me afford the condo, but that benefit came with the unfortunate consequence that my husband also decided to move back to Dracut to be near us.

We had an ugly divorce—him disputing every detail and continuously taking me to court trying to reduce the amount of child support he had to pay. At that time, the courts required him to pay less than eighty dollars every two weeks toward Krista's care, but still, he challenged every penny. I couldn't go anywhere without him stalking me. And at one very low moment, he attempted to run off with Krista. She was staying at my older sister's house one evening when my brother had invited me over to play cards and try to take my mind off my emotional distress. When Krista saw her father, she ran to the door and opened it, and he grabbed her, yelling that he was taking her to California.

I called my lawyer, who instructed me to meet him at his office the next morning. Together, we went to court in Boston to arrange a restraining order, and then, with a police escort, we delivered the order to my husband's parents' house, where he and Krista had stayed overnight.

I got my daughter back that morning, and for some time thereafter, my husband's visits with Krista had to be supervised by his parents. Still, he found ways to threaten me—including sending home nasty letters tucked into Krista's bag giving voice to his rage.

I'm still horrified recounting just those few details from that time. But I need to mention them, because leaving that marriage was how I got started on the path to pursuing my happiness. Krista and I had our own place. I had my own car, and I had a job to support us. That was enough.

In the evenings and on weekends, I continued to sew window treatments. At first, I was sewing for people at the company, but then word-of-mouth recommendations helped spread requests for my services. We had a two-bedroom condo, and I had the sewing machine set up in my bedroom. I would lay out the fabric on the floor and then contort myself maneuvering around it so that I could get the measurements and cuts just right.

As I thought about how I wanted to build my new life, I remembered sitting in on a window treatment seminar for interior designers, held at the Boston Design Center, the year before Krista was born. I'd made a point of seeking out the opportunity to hear what this superstar custom designer had to say even though I was very aware of not belonging to the crowd gathered there. The room was full of luxury designers, intimidating and unfriendly women dressed to the nines and carrying their French market baskets filled with fabric samples. Besides awareness of my own discomfort, what had stuck with me from that event was the speaker's claim that there was an increasing need to pivot from luxury and formal design to a more family-centric model. The other women in the room were quietly aghast at the message, but I had been thrilled by the speaker's assessment. Now that Krista and I finally had our condo, my primary goal was to make it reflect our little family.

My first DIY project was to rip up the linoleum in the bathroom— all the way down to the subfloor, which I then sanded, painted, and coated with polyurethane so that it looked like marble with a wide black border. Next, I took out the wall-mounted medicine cabinet and hung an old mirror with a black frame. Finally, I sewed a new shower curtain. There was pink carpeting in the living room and more ugly linoleum in the kitchen, so I worked on transforming those next. Not long after, while out antiquing in hopes of finding some cheap furnishings, I spotted a black fake-wood mantel with a metal back and plastic plug-in logs for fifty dollars. Krista and I didn't have much furniture in the condo, but I bought the mantel thinking we could have a "fireplace" to hang our Christmas stockings on. I decided to paint it white and put mirrored cut glass on the back and candles in place of the logs. That piece has come with me to every home and studio I've had since I purchased it. I think of my fixing it up as the first real cementing of my design aesthetic of mixing old with new.

My first mantle now painted white and in the Lowell, Massachusetts, teaching loft.

Slowly, I was designing my own place on my own terms. There was no more "Hurry up, let's get the fancy new house finished so we can show it off to everyone we know." In my marriage, everything had been for show, but the condo was a space where Krista and I could be true to ourselves.

When it was time for filing taxes that first year after getting divorced, my husband was sitting in the room with me and my accountant but wouldn't share any information with us. I sat there crying, wondering how I was going to turn in a document that reflected our true circumstances. Weeks later when we finally finished, my accountant contacted me to say, "You're getting a refund, and you need to go on a vacation."

It seemed completely antithetical to everything that had happened in the past two years to even contemplate a vacation. But I followed the accountant's advice and booked myself and Krista a trip to a family Club Med vacation spot in the Bahamas where there were lots of activities for children. It was our first vacation—and our only one for years to come. My mother and father flipped out about the whole thing—from the very fact of the matter down to the detail of the two of us getting on a plane by ourselves and traveling to a foreign country.

I needed to be clear with them: "This is my life now. I am going to do what I believe is going to make us happy." I was still in my twenties, but I'd seen enough of how people lived to know that there's what people see on the outside—some combination of what we show of ourselves and what people want to see in us—and then there's what's going on inside. A lot of people are not happy with their lives—with what they spend their time doing or whom they spend their time with. But most of us don't get to see any of that. What I wanted, by contrast, was for our little family to feel whole—as close as we could get to having our outsides and insides reflect one another.

I was scared. I was excited. But mostly I felt that I needed to embrace this new reality and make the most of my independence. Taking that vacation to the Bahamas was a way of proving to myself that I could.

From then on, when Krista had school vacations and her friends would visit Disney or go on big trips with their families, I would do whatever I could to find something fun for us to do together at home. One vacation, I taught Krista how to ride a bike; on another we went to the beach, collected shells, and then painted them to make ourselves Christmas ornaments. In every instance, we were finding things to do that we could afford and that might become special and lasting memories.

Christmas seashell ornaments.

During those years, through all the challenges, I remember thinking about each job, each project, each problem I had to solve as a stepping-stone on the way to where I wanted to be. And "where" I wanted to be was happy with myself—with my and Krista's lives. I sensed that there were people around me who wanted to tell me what I should be doing, who I should become, what was the "right" path to take as a newly divorced twenty-something with a little girl. To me, that advice felt laced with negativity, burdened by assumptions about our limitations. Much as the people who offered me their opinions about what we should do may have been trying to protect us from harm or even help us succeed, I didn't appreciate the dour pessimism of their recommendations.

Did I question my decisions? Heck, yes. But I also had a feeling—that grew stronger over time, like exercising a muscle—that I didn't care what other people had to say. I *needed* to make a life that was right for me, and so others' opinions and advice would have to be set aside when they weren't contributing toward that goal. This was my life with my child. Period.

I was a single mom with a clearer vision of the direction I wanted our lives to go, and I was willing to shed whatever negativity was going to hold us back. I think having consciously made that decision at a relatively young age helped me find ways of making the best of whatever we faced. I had my daughter when I was twenty-four; I was divorced and out on my own at twenty-seven, but instead of stopping me, those details of my life drove me forward even more steadily. Specifically, they raised some very practical issues I needed to figure out. How was I going to afford a mortgage? How was I going to send Krista to school, then to college? These questions didn't deter me from thinking about what would make me happy. Instead, they gave that question powerful focus.

I suppose having my daughter was the first of several turning points in my young life. I realized that I didn't want to go back to the corporate world and climb any ladders there. I *would* go back—because I needed steady employment and health insurance—but my goal was no longer to be successful in that arena. Instead, I wanted to have time with Krista, make space for being creative, and get paid. To me, that's what it meant to say, "I'm not going to settle."

And to do that, I needed to find my own way. My top priority was supporting my daughter and getting her through whatever I needed to get her through. I had no help from Krista's father, and that was fine. I would make it work. By working in the corporate world in the daytime and working at night designing and sewing window treatments, I *could* make it work. I always had a vision of how I wanted to spend my time and how I wanted to feel about my life. I wanted to move toward being self-employed. And I wanted to know what it would be like to have my own design studio.

I'll be the first to point out that I had no more sophisticated a plan than that—no five-year maps or short- and longer-term goals for business growth, for training, for networking, or anything of the sort. I may not have known precisely how I would afford to send Krista to college. But I knew that I would do that for her, no matter what.

So, when I suggest the importance of finding a path and getting on it, I mean both determining what is right for your happiness and formulating at the very least a general vision and overall plan. I'll add this important note regarding planning of any kind: it's often the case that one's life circumstances are always and forever changing in unexpected ways. Nevertheless, I think knowing what you have a love or passion for and taking steps in the direction of that passion keep the possibilities associated with it always flickering in your brain. That flicker generates others and can build and build until you've created a whole world of your own—sometimes without even realizing all you've done.

In one sense, planning is as simple as keeping going in the direction of what you feel will make you happy with your life. Doing that may take you places you didn't know to expect. There may even be some wonderful surprises along the way that illuminate in greater detail precisely what you need. But if you want to incorporate what you love into your everyday activity and into a source of income, you have to pick a path that you think might take you there and then get moving.

Especially when you're facing hardship along the way, it's important to keep in your mind that vision of what's going to make you happy. At one point, I was working four jobs at once, but all of them were related to the interior design industry in some way—they fit with my overall vision. I didn't care if I was mixing a can of paint or hanging wallpaper. I just wanted to learn, to get some experience, and I didn't know which one, or ones, of those different avenues I was trying out would turn into something just right for me.

I've seen a lot of people wanting to change their lives and their career trajectories who believe they can't because they can't afford to go back to get four-year college degrees or other specialty training, or they can't afford to quit their current jobs for ones that pay a lot less but might be more satisfying. Anticipated cost is probably the number one reason a lot of people turn away from their curiosity about alternative paths.

I want to suggest that focusing on the monetary costs of the change we want to make is one of the most convincing ways that we set up obstacles for ourselves. If you want to do something that's going to make you happy, there will always be alternative paths than the first ones—or the easiest or fastest or most expensive ones—you imagine. There are always other avenues to take. The important thing is committing to taking the journey, believing that it's worthwhile, getting on that path in some way or other, and seeing where it goes. What other opportunities will you come across? What else might you learn about what you really enjoy? How will your goals be refined by moving yourself in the direction of what you love?

I fully realize that besides ginning up the courage to strike out on your own path, dealing with financial concerns is the most difficult obstacle precisely because those concerns can feel like a great weight and because striking out on our own usually challenges our ability to feel as if we can carry that weight. Even now, when I talk with people who seek out my courses, I can't give them a comforting answer to the important question "If I complete your course, what position am I going to be qualified for? What is this going to get me?"

I can't answer that question for good reason. Nothing is going to fall into your lap after you complete a training, get a degree, or develop a skill. Likely, no one is going to be there at the end of the process to acknowledge your effort to live your best life or reward you with a good job. A lot depends on initiative and your willingness to push ego aside in order to take baby steps toward your goal. A lot depends on having a reasonable amount of faith that stepping onto your path and getting moving can lead to something better. It requires effort, and discomfort is likely.

Staying open to what you discover is a big part of moving yourself forward in the direction of your creativity. Along the way, it's worth remembering that there are different ways of incorporating your passion or your hobby into the way you earn a living.

Every one of my students is eager to explore their love of interior design, but they are often surprised when they discover their niche or special talent. One of my students ended up pursuing photography after enjoying the exercise we do in class on taking before and after photos of our work. Just starting down the interior design pathway led her to discover that what she really enjoyed was taking these photos. She got started without necessarily knowing just where she was headed. But she could at the very least name the industry in which she wanted to work. So, she found a way in and has since turned that into steady work.

Staying open to what you discover is a big part of moving yourself forward in the direction of your creativity.

To me, that's as good an argument as any for trying any and all the things that make sense to try. When you're doing something you enjoy, it gets easier to discover what else, or what part of that, you like and are good at. People don't just start out knowing everything about the niche they might enter or establish. They start by trying something they're curious about, then push aside their own naysaying. They switch out statements like "That's going to cost a lot of money" and "No one is going to hire me to do that" for ones like "I'm willing to try this because it interests me" and "I want to walk on a path that I choose and create for myself."

I promise you, some version of what you'd like to do can be done. You don't necessarily need special schooling or a big savings account. But what you do need is that bit of courage. You'll need the courage to identify what sparks your interest and enthusiasm. And you may need the courage to think outside the box about how to step in that direction.

I needed to get out of a bad marriage and away from an increasingly abusive husband. I needed to support my daughter through the early decades of her life. I was going to do what it took to find a way forward. I didn't need to know exactly where I was headed, but I had some idea.

Then, I had to think carefully about budgets and finances. For me, the more I went forward toward making a career in interior design, the more—not less—I thought about how I could return to a job in the corporate world if I needed to. I

Some version of what you'd like to do can be done. You don't necessarily need special schooling or a big savings account. But what you do need is that bit of courage.

would work as a secretary if that was required. My vision was always at the forefront, but I didn't have so much pride that I imagined not needing to return, along the way, to sources of income and skills I could rely on.

I don't know anyone who's left their day job with the plan, "I'm going to paint pictures now, and people will pay me thousands of dollars for them." Nearly every one of us has to figure out how we are going to pay for our lives. Ultimately, that involves at least some planning.

I was already making window treatments when I decided to move toward the goal of opening my own design studio, but even a relatively steady stream of window treatment clients wasn't going to be enough to pay for a mortgage and electricity, groceries and clothing and a vehicle, let alone some fun things like my daughter joining the softball team. For me, planning meant answering basic questions like these: Are we going to need day care services? Do I need to work part time because I have to be available to take Krista to school in the morning and pick her up in the afternoon? What does private school cost? How much do I need to earn each month? Who are the people I consider part of my support system, and in what ways, specifically, can and do they support me?

When I left my husband, I couldn't afford to buy a ten-dollar pair of shoes. But I also knew in my heart that I couldn't afford to live with someone who smothered me and showed contempt for my every creative impulse.

I knew, too, that I could rely on my family. That was a big part of what allowed me even to think about taking steps in the direction of my real interests. Krista and I could live with my parents if we needed to. My parents could watch her three days a week, and I could send her to day care two days a week. My family was an absolutely necessary part of my support system.

Most of us aren't in situations where we can just take a wild leap in the direction we desire on the assumption that everything is going to work out well for us. There will be hard work. There will be times when you may feel like you're focused primarily on survival. We all need to make money. The challenge I'm proposing is figuring out how to make money doing something you love. Most all of us have to choose from among what options are available to us at any given moment. And if we find ourselves having to choose something that's not going to move us toward our dreams, then it becomes all the more important in those moments to find creative ways of keeping our interests and our practice alive.

In my own story, sewing has been both a through line and a lifeline. I made my daughter's clothes. I made window treatments for myself and then for other people. I kept sewing and finding ways forward, even when I didn't know just where they would lead.

Dresses made for Krista by Debbe.

Chapter Three

VISUALIZE YOUR OPPORTUNITIES

*I*n practice, visualizing opportunities can feel as if it has two sides. On the one, there is the creative work of establishing a big vision for your life—your long game. On the other, there is the business of imagining and determining each of the steps along the path toward that goal. In my own experience, I've noticed that taking advantage of opportunities to accumulate steps requires being open to gaining experience in whatever forms it presents itself. In other words, a bit of a balancing act exists between on one hand picturing something big, bigger maybe than you—or those around you—have allowed yourself to picture and on the other hand recognizing that no step toward that goal is too small or insignificant to pursue. We just can't tell ahead of time what the full significance will be of any action we take.

Before I took my first big step—which was starting a design studio with my sister-in-law in the early 1990s—I worked that part-time gig selling fasteners. On its surface, that experience may not seem like it was much of a stepping-stone along the way toward my big vision, but it turns out that from working that job, I discovered a love of power tools that has stayed with me—and helped me in my business—to this day. The familiarity I developed with a drill also allowed me to feel more confident renovating our condo; it helped me understand in greater detail just "how" the work I envisioned would get done.

A balancing act exists between on one hand picturing something big … and on the other hand recognizing that no step toward that goal is too small or insignificant to pursue.

Eclectic Expressions, our interior design studio, lasted five years. From the start, my sister-in-law and I did not share the workload equally, even more so when she got pregnant with my nephew. I also learned that everyone loves when you're in business, because they want to take advantage of your discounts and your access to wholesale vendors. When it came time to do our taxes that first year, I ended up getting into a dispute with my brother over deductions on our tax documents. This was heart wrenching for us both, as our relationship was otherwise so close.

My sister-in-law dropped out of the business after a couple of years, after which I tried to do it all myself: design consults, window treatments, stocking the store with antique pieces I'd find while thrifting. Krista would get dropped off at the shop after school and spend time making her little shell ornaments that we sold for a dollar apiece.

The first two years that we had Eclectic Expressions, I also worked several evenings a week and on Saturdays at a flooring retail store. There, I learned tile, carpet, and hardwood and got to work with people who were building new homes. I made a lot of client connections at the flooring store. When clients came in to pick out their flooring, they'd begin by looking at builder-grade products. But they never ended up with that when I was there to help them. They'd bring in pictures of what they really wanted, and I started doing little design consultations for them. I'd go with them to their new space, we'd pick out flooring as well as their paint colors, and projects would just evolve naturally from there.

The rest of my business came from word of mouth and from advertising in the Valpak—a direct-mail marketing operation in which I could include a little discount coupon.

In my initial Valpak offering, I branched out from promoting soft window treatments to include hard treatments (blinds and shades), and I was excited to go out and take measurements for the first client who ordered those. Getting the measurements right is tricky, and I got them all wrong. My dad, the engineer, had always tried to teach us kids math. He'd gather us at the dining room table for little lessons, and from early on it had been clear that I wasn't a math person. But let me tell you, I learned everything I needed to know about measuring from this one costly mistake. My brother, the other engineer in the family, had agreed to go in and install the blinds for me and was the one to point out that I'd measured the blind track bigger than the space available for it. I had to eat that cost.

I had put myself out there as a professional claiming knowledge about window treatments, but I still had to learn from trial and error—and from calling up my father so that he could explain to me the significance of a sixteenth of an inch. Just putting my name out there was itself a big step—and I might have come away from that early experience thinking that I should stick to making soft treatments only or that I should always hire someone else to come in and measure for me. Instead, I decided to learn how to measure correctly every time.

During that same period, I had to make some decisions about the path of my personal life. I didn't socialize or date after the divorce; the time I spent outside the condo was for work, for Krista's school events, and for dinner at my parents' house. My first cousin was the person closest to me who decided to do something about the fact that I was shying away from friendships and fun. She called me up on a Friday afternoon: "All right, Debbe. This is what's going to happen. Gina is going to watch Krista, and you are going to go out with me and my friends and then sleep over at my place."

I couldn't imagine it.

"We are having a sleepover, Debbe. Meet us at the apartment. We'll have a drink, and then we're going into Boston, and you are going to have fun."

She was determined.

We hadn't been out at the bar for long before a very handsome man asked if I wanted to dance.

At the end of a fun night of dancing, he asked, "So, are you going to be back here next weekend?"

"No. I am not. I don't go out very often."

"Well, could I have your number?"

I gave it to him on the assumption that no one I'd meet at a nightclub was actually going to call me afterward.

"If I call you, you have to go out with me on a date," he teased.

"Sure."

When he called, I felt the need to explain. "I really didn't think I'd hear from you. I have to tell you a little bit about myself. I'm divorced, and I have a four-year-old daughter. I'm not used to going out with people or dating."

He still wanted to date me, and four years later, he decided to move from Boston to Dracut. He bought a house, and after a few years, I rented out the condo, and Krista and I moved in with him. Then a couple years more after that transition, I decided to sell the condo. He wanted us to invest together in a ski house up in the mountains, but I refused. "I'm not married to you. I'm not buying anything with you." So, he married me, and we bought a little vacation home in the mountains—just the sort of fixer-upper that I could get excited about.

Jack was great, and he was good with Krista. But I entered that marriage with the thought—sometimes in the front of my mind, sometimes further back—that Krista was my responsibility only. He was a friend to her, but he wasn't financially responsible for her. And he would never be her father.

After a while, I got busy enough at the studio to hire a woman who could help me sew treatments. My younger sister Gina, who was in college by then, worked part time doing my books. And I continued to build my confidence as a professional by taking night courses at the New York School of Design. Each of these things felt like progress, but I was also finding it more and more difficult to have a shop and be a single mom. I wanted to be more involved with the parent-teacher organization in Krista's grade school, and I wanted to be finished with work appointments by a certain time on weekday afternoons so that she didn't have to get dropped off at the shop every day.

I decided to close the storefront and run the interior design business out of our house. That meant disassembling the showroom, selling off some of my antique pieces and some of the fabric and wallpaper books, the blind and shade displays, and other items that wouldn't fit into the space at home. I had a room upstairs that I used for an office, where I could set up all my samples, and a little sunroom just off that space for the fabric books that I was able to keep. I would still work and have appointments, but I could be home for Krista after school.

In 1996, I shut down my solo work and took a job at a local design center. They sold window treatments, flooring, wallpaper, and custom furniture. The owners were a husband-and-wife team, and the husband called me up and invited me to work full time as one of the design center's senior designers. "We're adding designers to our staff, and you were referred to me by someone who knows your work."

We talked for a while, but I couldn't see myself working full time. "Thank you for calling me. But I'm sorry, I'm just not interested in full-time work right now."

The next day, I heard from one of the design center's senior designers, Kathy, calling to persuade me to join the staff.

Days later, I decided to call back the owner. "How about part time?"

"Whatever you want."

"Okay. How about if I work one night a week and on Sundays?" That arrangement would still give me plenty of time with Krista.

Later that day, I got a follow-up call from Kathy. "Debbe, I understand you're coming to work here."

"Yes."

"Well, I just want to tell you how great a place this is to work. We're all looking forward to you joining us."

What appealed to me about that job was the opportunity to make myself even more accessible to people in the industry and to clients. Running my little shop, I had met some people, but that had grown more difficult when I started working from home. At the design center, I could position myself to meet and work with so many more.

The design center started out for me as an intimidating place to work. There was already a team of other designers there, and many of them found ways to express their suspicion of my capacity. I hadn't participated in the local or regional design community as much as they had. I'd had a little boutique retail studio and my own workroom for a while, and I'd done a little advertising here and there as I could afford it.

But the design center is also where I came to see just how all the different, small-seeming opportunities I'd sought out or taken advantage of had come to play a role in moving me forward.

As soon as I started picking up clients at the design center, I realized that I *did* have an established network—quirky as it was. I had the woman who helped me with window treatments and a person who upholstered furniture for me. I knew all the wallpaper and fabric and flooring lines, and I had established relationships with their sales representatives. I also knew how to measure for window treatments (soft and hard) and order my own fabric—two things the owner had to do for each of the other designers. By then, I had even done a bit of installation work myself and acquired a professional installer. I had my own whole network.

The other thing I learned working there was that I wasn't so much working in a retail showroom as I was working in something more like my own very large boutique showroom. Yes, we were open to the public, and people could come in and buy wallpaper rolls right off the floor, but more often than not, I was creating custom designs with access to a wide range of materials.

I was an asset to the place, and the owners paid me as such. Any problems I faced came directly, and indirectly, from Kathy, the queen bee of the group. She'd snooped through my file in the office and saw that I was being paid better than her from the very start of my employment. The reason for my high starting rate? I didn't need any training.

The result of Kathy's snooping was a considerable amount of animosity toward me, not only on her part but also from the other employees with whom she was close. They decidedly didn't like me at all. It didn't help that I made a lot in commissions, both from the people I brought to the design center and from new clients I met there.

Thankfully, there was Frank—the only male designer in the shop—with whom I became close friends. We worked on Thursday evenings and Sundays together, and he was a hoot—humorous, charming, and as excited about antiquing as I was. On Mondays, which we both had off work, we would go antique hunting together and compete to see who could get the prize piece or the best deal. He and his partner spent time with our family, and Krista adored them both.

When Krista started high school, I shifted over to full-time work at the design center. Besides the time I spent with Frank, the job was increasingly filled with tension and stress. It was a very busy environment, and the owners tended to argue—quite loudly, and with lots of swearing—whenever something went wrong with an order. Once I was working full time, I started to feel more and more that this wasn't the environment I wanted to be in—these weren't the people I wanted to spend so much time around.

It was during my sixth year working at the Design Center that I acquired a client who helped change the trajectory of my career. He came in with his wife to discuss their plans for remodeling a lakeside camp they owned. She had terminal cancer, and they wanted to sell off their big house and transform the camp into a year-round home where he and his ninety-year-old mother could live comfortably. I went with them to the camp for our initial consultation. Three weeks later, we had another appointment so that I could present them with options for flooring, area rugs, window treatments, paint, custom furniture—just about everything they needed to make that camp into a comfortable permanent home. The man brought his daughter to that second appointment. His wife had already passed away.

They were such a graceful and admirable family, and so strong to be able to prepare for death and handle it in the way they had.

The man and his daughter ordered everything. My bosses were the ones who went out to the property for the installation; they always delivered furnishings themselves in order to save a bit of money. It was pouring rain the night of the install, and the wife had to call her husband, who was already at the house, multiple times as she struggled to find her way on the dark streets of Westford, Massachusetts.

From what I knew of the clients, I could picture the gentleman and his mother calmly waiting in the house, some classical music playing in the background—as was the case on the two occasions I'd visited. Then I pictured my boss standing in their foyer, yelling and swearing at his wife for being lost on a nearby street.

The client had asked me to come by the next morning to see how everything looked. It was a bright and sunny morning, and when I stepped inside the house, it looked absolutely beautiful.

"Debbe, you are amazing. You have this gift," he started. "But I want you to sit down for a minute. I would like to tell you something."

That's how I found out about the evening before—the chaos, the swearing, the man's ninety-year-old mother sitting in her chair taking it all in.

"It is just unacceptable," he said, kindly and calmly.

I was mortified.

Then he asked, "Debbe, why are you working for these people?"

I don't remember what I said in response, or if I spoke at all.

But in that moment, I felt the full force of all the frustrations that had been building up in me about the group of people with whom I worked.

I got in my car and decided then and there that I could do this same work on my own, again. I went back to the design center and into the back office and sat down with the owners.

"The house looks great," I began, "but I have decided that it's time for me to leave here and venture out on my own again."

"Why is that?"

I said something vague about it just being time to move on, how it would be better for the both of us.

"And where are you going?" Either they did not believe me, or they imagined that I was taking work at a competitor's shop.

"I'm not going anywhere. I'm just going to do this thing myself. I'm here to give you my two weeks' notice."

They were not happy, but they agreed to it.

By the next day, they'd changed their minds. "You know what? You can leave today. We don't need you for two weeks."

"Okay."

"I don't think you have that much outstanding commissions or vacation time built up."

I had lots of both.

From having to face my first husband in court on the regular, I already had a lawyer. He wrote them a letter, after which I received my commission and the payout for my vacation time.

I couldn't have felt better about the decision. All the different jobs I'd taken and all the struggles—even my first marriage—had prepared me for that moment. I was in my mid-thirties, Krista was happy and doing well in school, I was in love with Jack, and I felt that all would be good for us going forward. Those years at the design center had shown me that I did have the skills to succeed and had given me the confidence I needed to venture out on my own again. I had the sense that I knew who I was, and I was ready to embrace the independent career I'd always envisioned.

Chapter Four

DIVERSIFY TO FIND YOUR NICHE

After quitting the Design Center at the Mill and starting up on my own, I worked from home, as I'd done before. I also grew curious about two emerging areas, home redesign and home staging, and attributed my interest to the rise and success of HGTV network shows. I decided that those might be good skills to add to my portfolio, ones that would both spur my enthusiasm and keep my business relevant as people's interests and needs changed.

There were a handful of programs across the whole of the US that were affiliated with the organization Interior Redesign Industry Specialists, or IRIS. One of those was an intensive certificate program nearby in Connecticut offered by Ann Anderson.

I shared with Jack my idea to enroll.

"Why would you waste your money on that?"

I hadn't expected this response.

"You already failed once at having your own business. What kind of money do you think you're going to make rearranging people's stuff?"

It didn't matter the tone with which Jack had delivered his verdict. It was the words themselves that cut.

So far as I saw it, I hadn't failed by starting my own shop as a single mom. I'd closed the shop because I chose to invest more in my daughter's life at a time when I believed she needed me to be present.

I thought about how Jack and I had merged our lives—falling in love, investing in property together—and how we hadn't; besides the properties, our financial lives were separate, and when it came to responsibility for Krista, I was the sole provider. Krista was always and only mine, and frankly, I'd grown comfortable with Jack not taking on any responsibility for her education or extracurriculars or other needs. Her father had remained a negative presence and an irritant, challenging me, as she grew, about child support, health insurance, and even Jack's role in her life. It seemed easier for me to be the only one of us making decisions about the costlier aspects of her care.

I viewed sticking with interior design as the way forward in fulfilling my responsibility to her. I didn't want to return to the corporate world, and I had reason to believe that I could make more money in interior design if I put my nose to the grindstone and built a solid career on my own. Going back to school for credentialing in redesign could help ensure that everything would be okay for me and Krista as I returned to working for myself.

I *had* to make it all work out, because I was determined to afford the education my daughter wanted and fund her ability to do with her life whatever she chose to do.

I'd needed to leave my first marriage so Krista and I could open up our lives to the possibility of happiness.

We had made some progress. And I wasn't going to turn our backs on that achievement.

Regardless of what Jack said and the sour taste it placed and left in my mouth, I decided that I was going to move forward with my plan.

It wasn't until Ann Anderson came into my life that I felt like I had a career mentor, someone who both understood the field deeply and offered meaningful and specific reinforcement for her students. She was the opposite of what I'd experienced starting out in the 1980s, when it seemed that no one who knew something about how the industry worked wanted to be helpful to those of us who didn't. Even when I took Ann's course—which started in 2003—it was still the case that any interior designers I met held their cards close to their chests. Ann stood out as the antidote to a long industry-wide practice of refusing to share business information or offer guidance to new designers.

She also offered a corrective to the various forms of naysaying that I struggled to shake off. Jack outright pooh-poohed my interest in expanding my skills, and my parents, much as they were willing to support me no matter what, were inclined to worry about my decisions and then make comments and suggestions born of their worry. But Ann welcomed and allowed me to express my creativity, and she gave me and her other students the tools to explore how to develop our livelihoods out of our talents and interests. Two things distinguished Ann's training: doing hands-on work (we learned by going into people's homes and creating unique spaces for them using what they already owned) and practicing the entrepreneurial skills necessary for building and sustaining a business.

When I finished Ann's program early in 2004, I felt excited, inspired, and supported.

I took what I learned from Ann and got right to work creating a monthly newsletter and collecting email addresses to expand the newsletter's audience. In addition to interior design recommendations, I usually featured a recipe and a gardening tip (or holiday tip, as the seasons dictated) and notice of upcoming events. That last element was key. If I could attract attention to the advice I offered in the newsletter, I could potentially also attract attendees to seminars and other small class offerings. I arranged a few presentations at our local public library in Pelham and sought out area groups like book clubs and garden clubs that might appreciate some advice from me. My first presentation at the library was called "How to Choose Paint Colors for Your Home," and about fifteen women attended—most of them stay-at-home moms. The women were excited to participate in the brief exercise I had planned for them, and I booked three appointments from that one presentation.

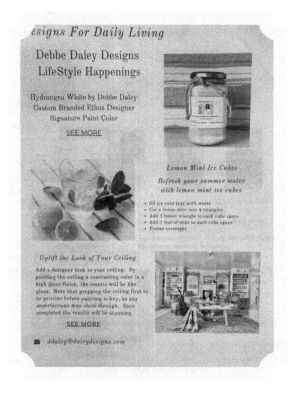

Newsletter: LifeStyle Happenings.

I learned from Ann that it didn't matter if the return on these initial efforts was small. I needed to remember that there was an audience. People *did* want what I offered. And at the time, almost no one else in the area was doing interior redesign or home staging—either in New Hampshire or on the East Coast generally.

The monthly newsletter planted seeds for the way I wanted to grow and the person I wanted to become. It opened up a lot of doors for me, especially insofar as those who received it and enjoyed it would then share it with friends. After a while, I started including focused offerings: a paint or a window treatment consultation—each for a set amount of time and a set price. Recipients were getting value from the newsletter tips, *and* it served as a free advertising tool. From the newsletter alone, requests for my services started to snowball. At one point, I was able to afford a business-card-size ad in two local newspapers, a move that brought in even more clients.

I started doing home staging for builders and developers in their model homes and writing a monthly design column for the *Merrimack Journal*. The editor of the journal had noticed that I advertised with them on the regular and offered me the opportunity to "write a little design tip" that would print each month. It was a generous offer in return for my business-card-size ad, and those little tips got bigger and bigger the more comfortable I got writing for the paper.

Merrimack Journal *article.*

Getting hired and being recognized locally for the work I was doing was amazing. I was learning to be true to myself, to do what I was genuinely interested in, and that kept me deeply engaged and motivated. I know there's a lot of talk about how we should all be true to ourselves, to really interrogate the extent to which we care about what we're doing. That's one thing in principle and another in practice. Honestly, I think it's surprisingly easy to forget what we're excited about and motivated by—particularly when we're already working in a field we like. Remembering to focus on what we *love* gets more difficult when we're already immersed in the work.

I've come to believe that clarifying one's niche—and thereby clarifying one's clients and one's general audience—has first and foremost to do with learning and evolving. In a sense, you position yourself within your industry by putting yourself out there in at least two ways: On the one hand, you try new things. We might even call that diversifying, but I'd say it's diversifying with a purpose—not for its own sake but with a curiosity about where your interests might take you. On the other hand, you do some straight and simple (and, whenever possible, free) marketing. If you sit at home behind your desk (whether literally or metaphorically) and don't work on meeting the people who might become your clients or your colleagues, you're not engaging in one of the most important activities that will position you in your chosen field.

I note these things because it took me some time to learn them ... and then to relearn them.

Clarifying one's niche ... has first and foremost to do with learning and evolving.

The timing of Ann encouraging me to focus on self-promotion couldn't have been better, because I needed to think seriously about supporting Krista through her years in college.

When Krista first started thinking about college and career, she imagined she'd become a dental hygienist. She was a kid who'd never needed braces, whose teeth were pearly white and perfectly aligned, and who loved going to the dentist. Then, she went to a college fair at her strict Catholic high school and had a moment of insight: "Mom, look at me! I'm wearing a uniform, but I've figured out how to style it in my own way. I love doing my hair and nails and makeup. I can't be cleaning people's teeth all day in a clean room situation. It's just not me!"

I agreed. It wasn't her.

She handed me some brochures.

"I think I want to check out a couple of these colleges with fashion merchandising programs."

"Okay, but if you do that, Krista, you're going to have to go to New York City. You can't do that anywhere around here."

I was both thoroughly excited for her and anxious all at once. *A fashion career in New York City. Whew. We'll make it work. Somehow, we will make it work*, I thought.

That may have been the first time I felt that same worry that I recognized my parents had expressed toward us kids. But no matter—I wanted to be different in that moment and not encourage Krista to choose something "more practical."

For April vacation the year she graduated from high school, Krista and I hopped in the car and drove to visit three colleges: Johnson and Wales in Rhode Island and FIT and LIM in New York. The Johnson and Wales program was good, but all its significant activities and field trips involved travel to New York City. It was obvious that her chances of success would be better if she were actually attending a program in the fashion district in New York. At the FIT open house, the guide emphasized the difficulty of getting accepted into the school's fashion merchandising program: "If you're not currently in tech school, or you are not taking courses right now in drawing or design, and you don't have a portfolio to show, it's going to be very difficult for you to find a place here."

LIM was different. It was a small, private college, and the open house was quite an event. They had coffee and breakfast treats for prospective students and their families and little gift bags for each person. Even the invitation to the open house had looked like it was announcing a special occasion. While we were there, each student got to have a one-on-one meeting with an advisor so they could pose whatever specific questions they had.

Krista got offered scholarship money at Johnson and Wales, was wait-listed at FIT, and got accepted to LIM.

We applied for financial aid at LIM, and that summer we loaded up Jack's Durango with nearly everything Krista owned—she insisted on taking all her things—and the two of us drove to New York.

At parent orientation, the deans warned us that a lot of students would struggle with city living: "Especially those students coming from a smaller town; the adjustment can often be very difficult." But Krista embraced the city. She thrived there and ended up staying another eight years after she finished her degree. She loved the culture, the restaurants, and her schooling, and LIM gave her the opportunity to work with the best in the industry. Once she got deeper into her coursework and internships, she decided on a major in fashion marketing. Her college years were busy ones—even on breaks, her degree program required her to work in different parts of the industry: manufacturing, design, retail, marketing, and the like. I was thrilled to watch her grow and thrive.

In a sense, Krista and I were finding and establishing our areas of expertise simultaneously.

Even though I was doing more than I had before—developing new skills and engaging more seriously in marketing and promotional efforts—I made sure I wasn't trying to do anything or everything. Frankly, just the thought of all the different things I might do was overwhelming! Instead, I made a conscious effort to do what genuinely interested me, what seemed as if it would help me grow and feel satisfied with my everyday work.

There's a lot of pressure to be engaged in every possible way and so to copy what everyone else is doing: "If *she's* got a podcast, then I need a podcast!" "If *they* use that expensive software, then I need to purchase that expensive software!" But here's the truth: Your success is not measured by the number of people on your staff, the variety of services you offer, or the number of media platforms on which you have a presence. No one of us needs to have all the fancy tools and do all the same things as everyone else—even our models and mentors.

After taking Ann's course, I was eligible to join the IRIS organization and the Interior Design Society. I got very involved in IRIS, and in 2006, I was invited to join the IRIS board of directors and give a presentation on home staging at their annual conference, which that year took place in Nashville, Tennessee. In preparation, I and my

IRIS colleagues Sandy Dixon and Debra Blackman put together a self-bound book we titled *Vacant to Vibrant*. In it, we shared our ideas about the ways that home staging could give empty properties their full advantage within the housing market.

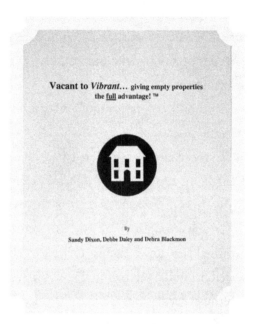

Our Vacant to Vibrant *self-bound book.*

What I remember most about Nashville was all the fun I had meeting other people who worked in the industry. After that long weekend, not only had I acquired several new friends but also felt that I had found my community—a group of people who were happy to support and cheer one another on. I had gone to other conferences before. But I'd been invited to speak at this one. And I got to meet and spend time with the keynote presenters—which felt both like a privilege and like an easy and completely natural thing.

When I think back on it, I see that I could not have predicted the series of dramatic changes that happened both in my career and in my personal life after that trip to Nashville.

I returned to New Hampshire feeling comfortable with my business but overwhelmed by having to take care of the properties that Jack and I owned.

When we first got married, Jack and I built a big house on two and a half acres in Pelham—right over the border from Massachusetts and about five minutes from my parents' house. We'd also acquired a house up in the mountains in Bartlett—a dilapidated little ski chalet that I styled à la one of Candice Bergen's cozy cottages that had been featured in *Architectural Digest*: distressed furnishings, hats and scarves hung on the walls for easy access, every detail communicating comfort and a sense of being at home.

That property in the mountains turned out to be a great place for us when Krista was in junior high and high school. We'd go up there on weekends, and she'd bring her friends. They'd ski and snowboard in the winter, tube along the river in the warmer months—just generally have a ball.

After some time, Jack got the idea to buy another property—this time, a lake house—to use as a rental. He found a place on Lake Winnipesaukee, another fixer-upper that we made into a quaint little haven.

Once Krista got her driver's license and lost interest in the mountain house, we were renting both places. Jack and I were each working a lot—him on his printing sales business and me growing my design studio—and caring for all three houses turned into quite a lot of work. Whenever it was time to turn over the rental properties, I ended up being the one to do it.

After I returned from Nashville, I took notice of something I hadn't quite acknowledged before. After all this time being together—the eight years we'd dated and the eight we'd been married—Jack and I had come to lead such separate lives.

I had my design studio upstairs over the garage; Jack had his printing sales business set up in the basement. He would end his workday at three o'clock in the afternoon and go to the gym until I cooked and served dinner around six. Dinnertime was a break in my workday but not the end of it, so Jack would pour himself a glass of Southern Comfort and 7UP and watch sports on TV in the evenings when I went upstairs to get back to my projects. If Jack wasn't at home in the evenings, I assumed it was because he had played golf in the daytime and gone out with his clients at night.

I realized after Nashville something else I may have known for some time: I wanted to downsize. Our home was much bigger than it needed to be, and the two additional properties we owned were more work than made them worthwhile. At least they were work for me, since we didn't share effort in the upkeep and since I didn't share in whatever profits there were.

I wanted us to grow together, not apart—to have the feeling of mutuality, of becoming something together, of sharing between us more than houses.

I might have responded to these recognitions by feeling stuck or miserable. But I was convinced that we didn't have to grow apart or have our marriage grow stagnant. Certainly, whatever patterns had developed between us were something that could be fixed. And I wanted to see about fixing them.

When I think back on it, I felt about our marriage a bit like I'd felt when I thought I might like to become a stockbroker. Something in my life was changing for the better, and I wanted Jack to move and change for the better with me. I didn't want the big house anymore. I didn't want to work on taking care of our rental properties. What I wanted was to work on *us*.

If there was a place I was interested in relocating to, it was the ocean—which was about forty-five minutes away from our primary home. Jack preferred the mountains, but he agreed to make a concession, if grudgingly, to indulge my interest in living at the beach.

When we pulled up to the first house we'd agreed to look at, Jack didn't even get out of the car. I went in alone and returned with a fully tied knot in my stomach.

We were both hungry at that point, so we stopped by an area diner.

I was the one to break the painful silence. "Jack, we've got to do something, because we're moving in two different directions, and I don't want that to continue." I paused, took a breath, and then added, "I want to get back to where we were before, and I want us to live by the ocean."

In saying those words, I was hyperaware of Jack's connection to my family, to our friends. He was very close with my brother, and my parents loved him. Everyone loved him. He had a lot of personality, and he was generally a good guy.

I went on. "You know, I really don't want the lake house anymore. I don't want the mountain house anymore. I don't even want the big Pelham house. Can we be happy with a smaller house, a simpler existence? Then we could just go and do the things that we used to do together all the time—you know, golf, skiing, rafting …"

"Yeah, I don't want to do that, Debbe."

I hadn't expected that the knot could tighten even more.

Jack went on. "I saw my parents miss all these opportunities in their lives. They never took any chances …"

"Oh. Wait … we're done? Are we done?"

For me, it was a new question, but Jack's answer was firm: "Yeah, I think we're done."

Being done turned out to be a slow process rather than a quick break. My younger sister Gina was getting married that fall, and I was hosting her shower at our Pelham house at the end of the month. But the even-nearer holiday was Father's Day, and Jack and I already had plans to spend that day golfing with my dad.

Father's Day morning, Jack and I were lying in bed before getting up. He took off my grandfather's wedding band and handed it over to me. We played golf, then went back to my parents' house for dinner.

They were dumbfounded, disbelieving.

After all, Jack was a good guy.

The following week, my parents came over to help clean the yard and the pool in preparation for Gina's wedding shower. Krista was home from college then, and all of us were outside except for Jack.

My father was the one to acknowledge his absence.

"Oh, he's in the house watching the Red Sox, Dad."

Krista chimed in. "Yeah, he's in there drinking his chalice of Southern Comfort and 7UP."

Our divorce was finalized in September, the day before Gina's wedding, which Jack and I both attended. We had the three properties together, but otherwise we hadn't ever mixed or shared money from our incomes and savings. Jack kept his printing business; I kept my interior design business. He wanted to keep the Pelham house and the lake house, so he bought me out of those, and we sold the mountain house. It was that simple.

Jack agreed that I could stay in the Pelham house until I found another place to live, so we lived in the same too-big house together for another handful of months after divorcing. We didn't really see one another. Our offices were still on separate levels. Schedule-wise, our paths didn't cross with any regularity, and I'd made a point of eating dinners at my parents'.

Not long after the Nashville conference, the IRIS organization had also fallen apart. Many of its members had gravitated toward the Real Estate Staging Association—RESA—but Ann Anderson and Kimberly Merrit decided to launch a brand-new organization—the Association of Design Education—and asked me to be one of the organization's education affiliates. That meant, among other things, that I'd offer a certificate course for designers interested in home staging. Ann and Kimberly also invited me to speak at ADE's first conference, in Springfield, Massachusetts, where I gave a presentation on marketing design businesses. My own business was increasing and keeping me busy at the same time that I started getting more and more engaged in professional development activities.

Our Greek church was in Lowell, Massachusetts, and one Sunday after mass, I went to the open houses downtown in old textile mills that were being refurbished and converted into lofts. Besides living near the ocean, I'd been enamored of loft living. When I was just starting out in the 1980s, I'd framed and kept on my dresser a magazine page featuring the loft space of a haberdasher. Lofts were the sorts of spaces I dreamed of living in but also never believed I would or could live in.

At the time, it was easy enough to make the case to my parents that I should purchase a loft in downtown Lowell. I was doing a lot of traveling and speaking, and I needed to be nearer to public transportation. I didn't want to rely on family and friends to drive me an hour from Dracut to Boston—and over the bridge from Dracut to Lowell during rush hour traffic—whenever I needed to catch a plane from or back to Logan Airport.

The American History Textile Museum in Lowell was on the first floor of a beautiful downtown space that was once, itself, a textile mill, and there were big banners out front of it promoting new luxury lofts on the floors above. I had no idea how much the lofts would cost, but I felt compelled to look at what was on offer.

I've mentioned that during this time I was building my business, doing what I could to exercise my entrepreneurial muscles. When I met the developer of the luxury lofts, he recognized me from a big spread that had appeared that same day in the *Lowell Sun* featuring the home staging aspect of my business. My photo was on the home page of the paper's Lifestyle section. "You're a celebrity!" the developer announced when he met me. He grabbed my hand and kissed my cheek and asked, "Did you see?"

I hadn't seen the paper that morning. "No, I just came from church."

"Well, let me show it to you!"

I was interested in a loft on the top floor, but those were already sold. "We're starting to develop the fourth floor," he said, already leading me there by the hand. At the time, the fourth floor was just a big open space. The windows were huge, and I had the option of selecting a space that looked out the back of the building with a view of the canal rather than a view of Main Street on the front side.

The property's ties to my heritage weren't lost on me. "The Acre," as it was called, had been one of Lowell's earliest ethnic neighborhoods, where Irish immigrants and then Greeks, Poles, and other eastern European laborers, among others, had built the canals and factories that had shaped Lowell into an industrial town. As part of a neighborhood renewal project, those textile mills and other properties downtown were being transformed into living and retail spaces.

The loft at ATHM before purchasing.

After: The loft looking into the design studio, with fabric wheel, living space, and the back acre of Lowell, Massachusetts.

There was no set plan for the loft, so I got to help design it right from the start. The developer had collected artifacts from the old mill, and he invited each new owner to select one to incorporate into their space. I chose a twelve-foot fabric wheel and asked to have it mounted on the ceiling in a big open space between the living and dining areas.

I visited the loft space once more before making a down payment and telling Jack that I'd found a place. Granted, it still had to be built out—none of the mechanicals had even been installed at the time I secured my purchase.

By early 2008, the developer was still extending the timeline for when the loft would be ready.

"Deb," Jack said to me one morning when we were both at home, "you're going to have to leave. I've got to get on with my life."

Crying, I called my father. "Dad, I have to get out of the house now."

"Okay, Debbe. I'll come up." I hung up from that call and started packing my things—all of them.

Jack was working in his basement office when my father came by to help me pack. My father just walked downstairs to chat with Jack—it was clear that my dad assumed they were still good buddies. In tears, I tried to reason with my father. "Dad. Why are you talking to him? We're not in love anymore! I've got to move on with my life."

"Debbe, we've got to find a solution."

"Dad, I *am* finding a solution! Now, help me take down these window treatments!"

This time, and unlike after my first marriage, instead of leaving with almost nothing, I rented two storage units and took most of the antique furnishings that I'd acquired during my time with Jack. My good friend Frank from the Design Center at the Mill had given me the crystal chandeliers from his and Michael's house back when they'd moved from Massachusetts to Florida. I loved those chandeliers almost as much as that mantel I purchased for fifty dollars so that Krista and I could hang our stockings that first Christmas we were alone together. All those items would move with me out of Pelham and into the new loft.

Though I'd wanted my relationship with my husband back, what I managed to get back were my chandeliers and antique furnishings, even the desk on the back of which my grandmother had taped my name. As before, what I wanted were the things that had meaning for me, furnishings that were significant for my family, items I'd made or purchased myself, and things that bore witness to my own life's transitions.

I meet a lot of people, women especially, who come to my classes or contact me with the goal of changing their lives midcareer or after a divorce or other trauma from which they've won themselves a new life. They have a good eye for design, and they think this field might be the path by which they move themselves forward.

My grandmother's desk in my loft design studio. It previously was olive green, and I painted to a distressed white.

I always begin by asking, "What is important to you?" and I don't at all mean that to be a frivolous question that can be satisfied by offering thoughtless answers. I want them to begin with a look inward and not outward at the potential group of people with whom they'll compete for business if they do go forward in the field. "What is important to you?" is the question I ask so that we can see about getting them started on a track that makes sense as a path toward their goals.

Is it money? Is it your relationship with your kids? Is it a place you'd like to live? Your spouse? Your family? A quiet life? A busy one?

Do you want to travel? Do you picture yourself socializing comfortably among a certain group of people?

We need to reveal the truly important things in order to see the path, to imagine what a given person might be excited to learn and who they might be excited to become. We focus first on what's important and then see what can be done to get there.

Even though I had a passion for design early on, even though I was family tutored and self-taught, I needed Ann Anderson to push the envelope a little bit, to introduce aspects of business ownership that I didn't know much about and to encourage me in the direction of my strengths. Now, I try to give that to anyone who comes to me looking for a mentor or to jump-start a career in interior design.

First, we have to find out about you—what you're good at and so much more than just what you're good at. To put it another way, we need to know what goes with you wherever you go.

For me, and by now you know, it's my daughter. Still to this day, she's my concern wherever I go. She's in her mid-thirties as I write this, but she's what's most important. And just the same, if no one is going to come along on your ride with you, it's good to know that, too. Some things—and some people—you have to leave behind if for no other reason than that you can't change what you have no control over.

For four months in early 2008, after Jack said I needed to leave, I moved out of the Pelham house and back into my strict Greek parents' home. I suppose I could have moved in with my brother and his wife, but they were such close friends with Jack—still hanging out with him and all—that it would have been terribly awkward for every one of us. Instead, I moved myself and my home-based business into my parents' basement—all the fabric books, the paint cases, everything I needed to keep working. My desk was right next to the washer and dryer—a true challenge given my mother's penchant for doing laundry at most hours of the day.

I was living and working in the very space in which I'd played house as a girl. More than once, I was on the phone scheduling clients when my mother yelled down to me, as she'd done so many years before, "Debbe! Dinner's ready! Deb, did you hear me? Dinner's ready!"

Chapter Five

MANAGING RISK

I moved into the Lowell loft Memorial Day weekend 2008. My father went with me to my storage unit, and I loaded up the U-Haul truck and used the mill's freight elevator to unload. Because I was the first person to move in on a floor that had yet to be fully built out, I was able to put all my furnishings into the unfinished space next door and move in at my own pace, allowing me to be methodical in setting up my new home.

I started dating the loft developer. We'd been working together building out the space, and when he learned more about how I intended to set things up so that I could carve out a design studio within it, he offered me, free of charge, a vacant retail space he owned downtown. It was close enough that I could walk there from the loft.

"Why don't you just take the space?" he offered, with a charming ease I'd quickly grown used to.

The retail space was already familiar to me. It was where in high school we would go to get our band jackets and our field hockey uniforms. I opened a little studio there and offered some interior design and home staging classes when I had the time. Later, when I was contacted by Middlesex Community College to teach interior design classes for them, the studio space proved to be a perfect location—a quick trip for students just across the canal from the college.

Again, my father went with me to the storage unit to pick up and help me move some furniture into the studio space. It was early in the morning—about six thirty—when we pulled into the alleyway behind the building. That's when we met Ricardo. Ricardo and his wife owned an Italian restaurant just down the street, and they lived in one of the fifth-floor lofts. Ricardo caught sight of us unloading my father's SUV and came downstairs to help. After he and my father wrangled a chair from the back of the vehicle, the two of them sat down and proceeded to chat like two old Greeks who'd just met up at a café.

I moved most of the rest of the furniture into the studio myself.

But after that morning, Ricardo and his wife became my go-to people in Lowell. Ricardo's was "the" restaurant in town and especially popular after a big event at the auditorium nearby. I would go there on the regular for dinner—just by myself—and spend time talking with them.

Ricardo introduced me to his best friend, Jim—the editor of the *Lowell Sun*. Their offices were just downstairs from my loft, and I'd been called on once by one of their reporters, Nancye, to offer content when she needed to write a design or decorating feature. The first year I lived there, Nancye even produced a little video of me offering quick—and affordable—tips on holiday decorating. We'd shot the segment in my loft, where I talked about how I liked to venture off into the woods and cut or pick pine branches to use as decoration—weaving them through the chandelier, wrapping them around columns, placing them just so to create tablescapes. After I got to know the editor Jim and his wife a bit, I called up the courage to ask Jim about writing a Lifestyle column. I'd stopped my column for the *Merrimack Journal* after the editor there passed away and the journal closed down, but I missed writing. When Jim said, "Well, let's set up an appointment for you to come down to my office and show me what you've got," my first thought was *Oh, God! I have an appointment with Jim! I need a portfolio!*

Thankfully, I'd made a binder of newspaper clippings.

"Deb, this is great stuff! Do you think you could do this every week? Do you have enough content?"

"Are you kidding me? I have tons!"

"Great. We're setting up a new series. We're gonna give you a videographer, and you can write a print column and blog in conjunction with that. We'll call it Daley Decor."

Just like that, I had a team of people following me around on my projects. It was great … until I realized that I still had a lot of work to do! When Jim proposed that we shift to a twice-a-week column, I knew I had to speak up. "Jim, I've got to work! I can't do my job and have a camera crew with me all the time waiting to see what's going to happen and deciding whether or not it's worth using. My projects don't get finished in a day."

Jim was kind and proposed that I take my own pictures. That arrangement worked much better, and what started out as a quarter-page column eventually turned into a half page and then a full page of the Lifestyle section every Friday. It was an amazing advertising opportunity for me. I was essentially new to Lowell, but through Ricardo and Jim, I'd been given opportunities to put myself out there and find an audience more quickly than I could have imagined.

The downtown studio was near a furniture showroom—Comfort Furniture—that had been a family business for over sixty years. When the father died, the son had taken over and kept the business going. I would bring my clients and my fabric samples over to their showroom to see and try out pieces from the lines with which I worked. I made friends with the sales reps who worked in the showroom, and I brought so much business to the store itself that at one point I was invited to have an office there. But my days at the Design Center at the Mill and my determination to succeed at having my own business helped me decide that this was one opportunity I would firmly decline.

I joined the chamber of commerce and felt as if my business was becoming a staple of the downtown Lowell scene. Ricardo introduced me to Sarah, a waitress at the café who wanted to learn interior design. She'd put her résumé in my studio mailbox a couple of times, but I hadn't thought twice about having an assistant—as much as I may have benefited from having one.

One evening at the restaurant, Sarah approached Ricardo. "Is that Debbe Daley?"

"Yes, it is."

Ricardo introduced us directly, Sarah came to the studio the next day for an interview, and I hired her. She was wonderful and organized, and after a while I started inviting her to do paint consultations with me.

In 2010, my relationship with the developer fell apart. That July, he took me on a surprise trip to Bermuda, and when we returned, I learned about all the other women he was seeing. Like most women, I would never have put myself in that situation had I been aware of his manipulations beforehand, so I quickly ended our relationship.

The very first thing I did was move my studio out of the space that he owned. That meant having to transform the loft into a partial studio. Krista's bedroom became the space for housing all the fabric samples and wallpaper books; there was just enough room to fit a desk in there for meeting clients.

The second thing I did was move to Boston. My father and I had a big argument about my decision. As he put it, "Why the hell are you wasting your money doing that?" But I needed to get away from that soured relationship with a man who was himself so embedded in the Lowell scene that I couldn't imagine being in it with him. I needed to step back and reassess my life on the one hand and keep it moving on the other. Boston seemed like just the right place for doing both. So, I found a tiny apartment and opened a little studio in the North End. I could take the train between Boston and Lowell as I worked to establish a business in the former and maintain my business in the latter.

The North End community was wonderful, but after a year filled with lots of socializing with my friends and eating all the delicious

Italian food so readily available, I started to miss the loft with its big windows. I realized, too, that the way my relationship with the developer had made me feel so unsure of myself—the fact that I'd so easily trusted someone I should never have trusted—had dissipated.

I hadn't been back in Lowell for more than a minute before Krista called from New York on a Saturday night. She was out having fun with her girlfriends. "Ma. What are you doing right now?"

"I'm back in the loft. I'm moving back in."

"Oh, good. But what are you doing right now, tonight?"

"Well, I'm using some power tools and building a staircase with stringers I ordered so I can make an upper loft."

"Listen. It's a Saturday night. You're home by yourself. I don't want to see you grow old and lonely because all you do is work."

"Okay, Krista. Okay."

"Ma, you're going on a date."

Her friend's father was also divorced and not seeing anyone.

"I think you'll really like him! He checked you out on Facebook, and he wants to go out with you."

"Okay, Krista. I get the message loud and clear."

We met up at a restaurant I'd chosen in Pickering Wharf, an hour from Lowell. I approached him and had barely said the word *hello* before he broke into a Rodney Dangerfield shtick with a comment about the way I looked. I knew how much Krista wanted me to get out, so I stayed and had dinner with him. At the end of the evening, he walked me to my car, and when I gestured toward giving him a hug, he proceeded to grab me and stick his tongue down my throat. That's when I decided I was good with being alone.

I had moved back to Lowell right around the time that the repercussions of the economic downturn started to take effect in the interior design world. During all that while, I worked out of the loft and kept up my close relationship with the Comfort Furniture showroom.

Then, in 2011, one of the sales representatives called me up, his voice agitated. "Debbe. I know you have a lot of orders here right now. But things aren't good. You'd better come down and see if you can get your clients' money back."

Besides a number of smaller orders, I had three big custom furnishing projects through Comfort, one of which was for a ninety-year-old client and family friend who'd spent quite a lot of money on pieces she was eager to acquire.

I went immediately to the showroom and spoke with the owner. He gave me the deposit back on one order I'd just placed and said everything else was on back order but should be available in the coming weeks. I believed him.

At the start of the next week, the sales representative I knew called back to say he'd been let go and that the company had hired one of those big firms that comes in to help liquidate bankrupt businesses. I went immediately back to the showroom, this time to ask specifically about the ninety-year-old client's pieces—all of them from the luxury brand Wesley Hall.

"You know her personally. Your father knew her personally. We need to get her money back!" I said.

"Debbe, I can't give her the money back, but she can come in today and pick something she likes off the floor."

I gave my client a call, and by the time she met me at the showroom, there were people taping kraft paper to the windows.

The infuriating thing was that the furnishings she'd ordered were sitting out back of the building on a delivery truck that arrived while we were in the showroom. I learned this because the office manager came out to the showroom to ask the owner to pay the $1,500 COD shipment fee. The owner didn't have any money to pay the bill, and so the truck would have to turn around and take the furniture back to North Carolina. While my client was looking for substitute furnishings, I called on one of the Wesley Hall sales reps to see if there was anything we could do. The problem was that the order wasn't in my name—it had been placed by Comfort Furniture, and because Comfort Furniture had an outstanding balance of $1,500 that it could not pay, the delivery company would not unload my client's pieces off the truck.

She wasn't interested in anything we looked at in the showroom, but in the end, she picked out a chair and a powder-blue loveseat with a dark walnut finish on the legs—both from Wesley Hall. That evening, under cover of night, they were loaded into a pickup, and one of the office managers delivered the two pieces to this woman's home.

I heard from the Wesley Hall rep a few days later. My client's furnishings had arrived back at the shipping terminal in North Carolina. I was thrilled that we might be able to resolve the issue … until he said, "And I can give them to you for this price …"

"Oh no. She's not going to pay any more money for that furniture. She's not getting back her deposit, and I already know she won't agree to pay more than what she confirmed when she ordered."

That client never received her furniture. In the meantime, I worked hard to see what could be done for my other clients who'd also made deposits on pieces they were increasingly unlikely to receive.

I called on representatives from Hooker Furniture, Uttermost, Currey & Company, and others. With each, I had to establish a designer account in order to be able to repurchase furnishings my clients were already expecting. In one case—a family for whom I'd been working on a whole first floor of furniture to better accommodate their kids' needs—I was able to reorder everything but their dining room table.

For each reorder, I charged the deposits to my credit card, knowing that I would not ask clients to reimburse me when they'd already lost their original deposits through Comfort.

While I was scrambling to help my customers and save my own business from ruin, I agreed to be interviewed by the *Lowell Sun* about the showroom's abrupt closing. I told the reporter how I was working to get at least some furniture for my clients. In print, that translated into something more like "Debbe Daley is helping clients get their furniture."

The next thing I knew, I was getting emails and calls from lots of other people who had placed an order with Comfort either wanting to yell at me ("Did you *know* that this was happening?") or believing that I might be able to help them retrieve either their deposits or their furnishings ("Are you a lawyer? I understand you can get us our furniture …")

I tried to help them.

I made calls to different vendors on behalf of people I didn't even know. There was a family who'd invested in a solid wood table and chairs from Canadel. The kids had been getting hurt sitting in old chairs that kept breaking, so the couple had saved their money to buy something sturdier and safer.

They'd paid cash for the new set, and I couldn't do anything for them.

I'd been happy to work with the folks at Comfort Furniture. They'd allowed me to use their showroom like it was my very own. Now, here I was, spending tens of thousands of dollars to take care of clients who'd made a down payment that could not be returned. If you can believe it, as I was putting every penny I had into keeping my clients happy and sustaining my business, I was also wondering if I should go ahead and try selling furniture directly by bringing some sample furniture into my loft to show clients.

I'd already had to establish designer accounts, after all.

I transformed my bedroom into a little furniture showroom—with one piece from each of the three companies with which I'd established a formal relationship—and built a tiny little storage loft inside my loft, hidden by a curtain and just big enough to fit a mattress for sleeping.

I had a mortgage to pay. I had Krista's college tuition and expenses. And Sarah was working for me a couple of days a week, so I had an employee to pay as well. Given that everyone was by then in the throes of the economic downturn, business was much slower than it had been before. So, I lived off my credit cards and used all of my retirement savings to pay bills. I hated doing that, but I was determined not to go out of business.

After a while, I did something considered verboten in the business community: I hired one of my longtime clients who was also a financial analyst to help me do my books. She worked with me two days a week to establish a firm plan. Her overall message was this: "You need to contact your creditors and get on a payment schedule." I had let bills accumulate without ever even looking at them, let alone communicating with my creditors. Once I contacted lenders and let them know my situation, we were able to get me back on track—granted, it would be a long track—to paying off my debt.

As someone who's been through that process, I can say that I don't use credit cards anymore except for travel expenses. I never want to find myself in that situation again.

If there's a lesson to be drawn from this period in my life, when on more than one occasion I felt that I couldn't see a clear way forward, it's that even at some of the lowest and most difficult moments, I refused to accept the status quo or give up the business I was so committed to keeping alive. I'd taken a risk starting up on my own again—and I'd stayed true to my goal even when the opportunity to slot myself into the Comfort Furniture operation was on offer.

My early experiences in Lowell—and perhaps because some of those experiences had been so perfect, so welcoming—helped me see, once again, that it was up to me to let go of negative people and situations. If I was truly committed to being on my own path, I had to be nothing less than my full self and understand that no one was going to help me out as much as I could help myself move forward.

Please don't mistake my point: I absolutely needed my friends, my family, the mentors, and the other people who offered their love and support during difficult times. But I also needed personally to invest in myself. Especially in those moments of crisis—the divorce, the romance and breakup with the developer, the threat to my business posed by the furniture showroom bankruptcy—I needed to be even more myself, so to speak, rather than try to meet anyone else's expectations of me.

Ironically, becoming more myself meant recognizing the force and influence of my upbringing. I wouldn't have incurred the amount of debt I did if I hadn't decided it was important for me to do everything I could to ensure that my clients got what they expected and were happy. I'd internalized a lesson from my parents: I needed to be responsible, and that meant doing what I could to make those clients whole. What was important to me was being someone that others could count on and respect.

If there's one constant in life, it's that things evolve and change, even when you're absolutely sure they won't. Experiencing such uncertainty during that early period in Lowell only increased my respect for my parents—their advice, their stability, the legitimacy of their worries, and even my father's sternness. They'd both come to this country poor, and my father worked three jobs and went to school at night to become an engineer.

They'd taught me that no matter what chaos there was around me, I needed to have a plan. When Comfort Furniture went under, I needed quickly to call my clients and tell them exactly what I intended to do on their behalf. I had brought them into that situation. It wasn't as if they'd gone to Comfort Furniture on their own to make a purchase. They'd come to work with me, they'd trusted me, and I was the one who'd taken them there. I needed them to know my plan for getting us all out of the mud. There was no time to sit and wonder what to do—there was just a problem in need of resolution.

If there's one constant in life, it's that things evolve and change, even when you're absolutely sure they won't.

Krista sometimes points out to me that as a family, we never sit and mope. When we are faced with a problem, we figure out what can be done, do that as best we can, and move on with our lives. Was I scared to use my retirement savings and credit cards to get me through a rough patch, not knowing where the next design job was coming from? God, yes. But I also knew I needed to move through those humbling life changes rather than throw my arms up in defeat or spend time wondering what everyone else thought of me.

Chapter Six

ACCENTUATE THE POSITIVE

s I kept writing and blogging for the *Lowell Sun*, and in order to generate fresh content, I started to include material that reflected the design-related activities I enjoyed. So, for example, if I went to the Habitat for Humanity ReStore to see what they had available, I'd ask if they wanted to be featured in an article, take some pictures and video, and then write about the experience. At the time, I was concerned with having fresh content for each of my scheduled posts, but looking back on it now, I suppose that's when I started featuring more and more of my own interests and personal projects alongside my professional ones. I was putting myself out there more—showing more of my own personality and my lifestyle—and people responded positively. I wasn't doing anything glamorous. I was just taking simple things and making them fun, and I was helping readers identify and try out things that they could do on their own. That really appealed to a lot of people.

Around that same time, I decided that while I appreciated my siblings always including me in whatever they did, I wanted to stop feeling like a third—or fifth—wheel. I felt I needed to find and prioritize ways to enjoy life that didn't involve tagging along with my family. I started taking little trips on the weekends as a way of branching out on my own.

I still felt a strong desire to have a place by the ocean, and that led me to check out fixer-uppers on Plum Island. The island had quite a few charming little bungalows that at the time I would have been just about able to afford. I even put in a few offers, but the housing market had already shifted to bidders offering more than asking price. That was something I just couldn't do.

But that also didn't stop me from looking, or from trying to imagine the design potential of any of the affordable options I found. I'd bring my plumber down there and cross my fingers that he'd say I'd found a workable fixer-upper. More often than not, he'd say to me things like, "Deb! This place has no mechanicals!" or "Deb! It's all sand down there!"

"Yeah, I know. But just see if the pilings are good," I'd offer back.

"Deb, you need to get a structural engineer in here!"

When I found a sweet little shack, I did just that. I went to the town hall and hired a structural engineer who sent out an old man with a jackknife to poke at the pilings and see if they were dry.

"Yeah, these've been here since the 1930s."

Fair enough. The place had been listed as a 1930s surf shack.

"These are still pretty good."

The shack was on the dunes of a reservation, which meant that no one could build in front of the place and block out the ocean view. But there was no electricity. There was no toilet. And the existing lighting fixtures were original to the house.

It was just what I wanted.

As I was considering making an offer, I went out on a date that a contractor friend of mine set up between me and a friend of his. When I mentioned my plan to put an offer on the surf shack, my date, Jamie, offered his opinion: "You don't want to live on Plum Island. I grew up in Newburyport, just a straight shot over the marsh. It's a mess out there. They don't even have functional public sewers."

"Yes, they do! When's the last time you went there? Because it's pretty awesome! I'm looking at old surf shacks and bungalows."

"You know, I have a bungalow in Portsmouth. Just bought it a year ago for its deep-water dock. The house itself could use some updating."

Our conversation went from comparing bungalows to comparing notes about owning our own businesses. Jamie had started his welding business in a horse stable and had worked hard to grow it into a significant enterprise with a team of about 150 guys.

We kept talking business all through dinner and even as we were walking to the parking lot afterward.

"Is that your car?" he asked, and then hopped into the passenger seat to keep talking.

Before he got out, he said something I found a bit presumptuous, even funny. "You know, the women I've dated haven't liked it that I have to travel a lot for work. Sometimes the traveling is really unpredictable. If there's an emergency, I might have to hop on a plane or get in the car and go immediately."

No problem, I thought. *I'm happy with my life, and I'm never giving up my independence.*

Jamie and I became fast friends, and whenever we were both free from work, we'd go out on his boat, go skiing, or do some other fun activity together.

The first time I went to see his house, I noticed that he had several guitars. When he picked one up and started playing and singing, I teared up.

I told him that I'd played the flute as a young person. I'd essentially broken my father's heart when I decided midway through high school that I didn't want to take lessons anymore. He'd invested in the instrument, in my lessons, and was proud of my ability.

We didn't have a lot of money, but my father always wanted us to have the best of certain things. He ensured that I had music lessons in the same way that he ensured we all had sturdy shoes for our feet—Buster Brown saddle shoes, to be exact. Growing up in Greece, he'd barely had functional shoes, so keeping us in Buster Browns had been a point of pride for him.

Something about telling Jamie that story and listening to him play made me want to get out my flute and join in. From that point forward, whenever Jamie and I were at his place, we'd have a ball conducting little jam sessions.

That said, I remained determined not to let anyone into my life—not even this great guy with his guitar and his bungalow in need of a designer's touch.

We'd gone out for dinner one evening when, out of the blue, Jamie said, "Debbe. My mother wants to know where I'm spending all my time when I'm not traveling."

My palms started to sweat.

"My parents would like you to come to their house for Christmas Eve."

I was looking at him like *Man, you have got to be crazy.*

He grabbed my hand across the table. "Debbe, I'm just asking you to go with me to Christmas Eve for Chinese food. I'm not asking you to marry me."

I'd definitely built some walls when it came to potential love relationships. Jamie wasn't at all like any other man I'd been with, but those walls had grown sturdy. I had a business to protect. I had a daughter to protect. And I had to take better care with my own heart.

I went to the Christmas Eve gathering and met his parents, his brother, and his brother's wife. They were all lovely.

It was Jamie who encouraged me to expand the furniture and furnishings part of my business. I'd grown frustrated working out of the loft and having just a few furniture samples tucked into one of the rooms. "Why don't you set up a store of your own?" he'd asked nonchalantly.

I rented a showroom space right on the main street in Lowell, and in the summer of 2012, R.A.W.—short for Refined Authentic Warehouse—Furnishings was born. At R.A.W., I followed my favorite aesthetic: mixing samples of new furnishings with antique finds.

The weekend before we opened the shop, Jamie and I were driving to a wedding in Dexter, Maine. We stopped at an intersection just across from a huge old antique barn. I looked over at him, wide eyed.

"Debbe, we've got to get to the wedding."

"Just five minutes?"

"Look at the size of that barn. That is not going to take five minutes."

Both the selection and the prices were unbelievable. I bought a ton of stuff, from farm tables to mantels and everything in between. Before we left, I wrote the owner a check for $700 and said, "I'll be back on Tuesday." We were four hours from Lowell, and I would need to rent a U-Haul so that I could transport in just one trip everything I'd purchased.

We launched the shop during the Lowell Folk Festival—a huge annual music, food, and art fest—and Jamie played his guitar as part of the opening reception. I hired back the client who'd helped me get my business finances in order, plus a woman I'd met at the local ReStore when I wrote an article about shopping there. And for the summer, I welcomed an adorable intern who was a high school student interested in design.

Every single item I picked up from that barn got sold during the shop's opening weekend.

Around the same time that we opened R.A.W. Furnishings, I got a call from the National Home Show inviting me to speak at an event they were putting on in our local arena.

"Yes, I can do that." I was confused. "But may I ask ... How did you get my name?"

"We called ASID, and they told us that you were in the Lowell area."

"Oh!"

I wasn't a member of the American Society of Interior Designers and couldn't help but wonder why they recommended me. So, I called them to find out.

"You're kind of an honorary member of this professional association. You are out there doing the work."

Of course, I joined ASID. As part of the National Home Show, I offered a breakout session on interior redesign and set up a vendor booth with vignettes featuring items from the store. I'd acquired a company van—my brother's company was selling off one of its vans, and I bought it for around $3,000—so it was easy enough to shuttle all the pieces to and from the show.

R.A.W. Furnishings turned out to be a fantastic venue for hosting events. I held client appreciation parties there, hosted group meetings organized through the chamber of commerce (I was part of the group called WISE—Women Inspiring Success and Empowerment) and even accommodated a conference for the Association of Design Educators.

Even though Krista had graduated college by the time I met Jamie, I'd become accustomed to believing that I wouldn't find anyone who would understand my responsibilities as a single mother and, along with that, would understand the ins and outs of my business life. Jamie had defied both assumptions. He could talk out the contours of a problem with me with the analytic intensity of a high school girl assessing her peer's motives. He talks with his business partner the same way, and they always emerge with a solution to whatever issue they're facing.

He also intuitively understood the pressures and responsibilities of different aspects of my life. From the first months of our relationship, Jamie had offered some of the most sound and wise business advice I'd ever encountered. So, when Krista came to me with a pressing business question during her second job out of college, I knew that Jamie was the person with whom she needed to speak. At the time, she was doing marketing for a multibrand showroom in the fashion district, and when the owner decided to close the New York City location and move those employees to the LA showroom, Krista refused to go to the West Coast.

She'd been organizing all the sales for the New York location and had all these great connections, so when the showroom went up for sale, Krista had the idea to buy it.

I couldn't help her with that.

But Jamie could. He'd done some amazing work starting his own business, especially on the financing side, and he was thrilled that I'd asked him to give Krista some advice.

I called him as he was on his way to meet up with me in Lowell. "Sure!" he answered. "Give me her number, and I'll give her a call now."

Later, when I looked out the big windows to the parking lot below the loft, I saw that he had arrived and expected to see him in the loft seconds later. I had dinner on the table, but Jamie stayed down in the lot talking business with Krista for an hour, covering in detail every step she needed to take to make a reality of her desire to own a business.

She did what he recommended, and she succeeded. And the two of them have been in conversation since. Whenever she's having a dilemma, he's the person whose opinion she seeks out after mine.

For my birthday one year, the client I'd hired to help with my finances bought us both tickets to the Massachusetts Conference for Women in Boston. The keynote speaker was Arianna Huffington, whom I adored then and still adore now. I was completely in awe of the story she shared. She ended her talk with the following remark, spoken genuinely to all eight hundred of us in the audience: "I invite any of you out there: if you write, or if you have a story to tell, send me an email."

So, I emailed her one Sunday morning a month or so after the conference. I told her a little bit of my story and my background and hit the send button before second-guessing myself. Jamie and I went out skiing for the day, and when we came back in the evening, I checked my emails in preparation for the coming week.

"Oh my God! I got an email from Arianna," I shouted from my desk.

Debbe, I would love for you to have a voice on the Huffington Post. I'm copying my creative editor here, and she will help set you up in the system so that you can start blogging when you're ready.

Honestly, it was that easy.

I wrote inspirational articles that combined design tips with personal reflections on being a working single mom seeking work-life balance. Arianna had recently released a book called *Thrive: The Third Metric to Redefining Success and Creating a Life of Well-Being, Wisdom, and Wonder*, in which she talked about having a job that required her to be constantly on the go and left her feeling like she couldn't take any time for herself. Following a sudden collapse from exhaustion, she'd changed her whole outlook on the meaning of success, and so her interest in stories of women trying for work-life balance was both keen and personal.

I moved into Jamie's Portsmouth bungalow and sold my Lowell loft in 2014. Jamie traveled a lot, and I was commuting back and forth between Lowell and Portsmouth as well as traveling for work myself. I'd be in Portsmouth from late Thursday to early Monday and then be on the road throughout the week. It made sense for us to live in the same place so that we could spend our downtime together.

It was a big step for me to let go of that loft. I'd purchased it myself, I'd helped design it, and living there, I'd built out my professional presence, become part of the Lowell community. I'd also grown more secure with myself while living there. Leaving was hard.

Jamie both recognized and appreciated my need for freedom. It frustrated him sometimes, but he also encouraged me to do things that would keep me feeling independent. One night that first summer after I sold the loft, I was searching through my Dropbox folders trying to locate the change-of-address form that I'd submitted to the post office. Not owning a place was already making me feel like I'd given up an important part of myself. Having a place of my own, having a vehicle of my own—these things had been markers, for me, of my own autonomy. I started having anxiety about not owning anything. I also didn't want to let go of the loft's furnishings, because I'd had my stuff taken away from me before and wanted to make sure that never happened again.

Jamie, sensing my unease, suggested I buy an apartment in Lowell that would still be mine alone.

"Debbe," he began, "you need to own something that's yours. I can tell. Why don't you go buy a smaller loft or an apartment that you can have just to yourself? It can be all yours, and it'll be perfect for when you go to meet with clients and you need to stay overnight."

So, I bought a little loft space in the building where my grandmother had worked in a shoe factory, and I felt better.

That fall, Jamie and I hosted both sets of our parents in Portsmouth for Thanksgiving. After dinner, and without any fanfare, he and I sat down together in the living room and started to jam. Krista was there, giggling, because she'd never heard me play the flute before. Honestly, I don't think she knew that I could play a musical instrument. I saw my father tear up, and I knew that this was one of the most beautiful gifts I could have given him.

In a handful of years, I'd come to think differently about Jamie's comment to me back when he sat in my car on that first date. His mention of past girlfriends being uncomfortable with his work travel hadn't been presumptuous so much as it had been vulnerable. He'd been shy about getting involved in a relationship, worried already on that first date about letting me down. He was telling me about a pattern in his own experience that involved falling in love and getting hurt in the end.

Our relationship developed slowly because each of us had wanted to take it slowly.

In those early years, Jamie made comments like "You know, if I were to get married, I'd want to marry you."

Huh, I'd think. *Why would you want to get married?*

When I think back on the relationships I had prior to meeting Jamie, I want to say that I got involved without thinking much at all about the big picture. I fell in love, followed my curiosity, and didn't really think far beyond the present.

But I'd matured since then. And I'd been divorced twice. And for each of those past relationships, leaving was an attempt to release myself from negativity—bold negativity, creeping negativity, all the different expressions of disapproval, of pessimism, of disinterest or disregard. Because I was shedding negativity coming from the very people I'd imagined would be supportive of me, moving forward always felt like something I had to do *by* myself and *for* myself and for Krista. Wanting to be happy had seemed—at some pivotal moments—like it required me to be a fierce protector of myself and my daughter and that I was the only reliable source of support for us both.

A similar dynamic had been true of my career. When it came to establishing myself as an interior designer, I'd felt quite alone for quite some time. If I wanted to pursue my passion, I had to make my own opportunities. There were no obvious or easily accessible sources of guidance. And all the resources that exist today weren't there—no groups offering encouragement and vital advice.

Stepping away from sources of negativity has been a big motivating factor in my life and a big driver of my career. But that's only the half of it. Identifying supporters, establishing communities, finding and using my voice—these have been essential positive steps along the way, the kind of steps that have helped shine a light on my actual path forward.

Stepping away from sources of negativity has been a big motivating factor in my life and a big driver of my career. But that's only the half of it. Identifying supporters, establishing communities, finding and using my voice—these have been essential positive steps along the way.

If there's a transition that took place for me during the years I spent in Lowell, it involved finding myself and my strength in ways that didn't simply have to do with letting go of negative influences. While there, I learned—maybe *remembered* is the better word—that there were people who were willing, some of them even eager, to support me and my dream.

Chapter Seven

SHARE WHAT YOU KNOW

In 2015, we expanded the space at R.A.W. by breaking through the wall and creating a design studio next door. That arrangement made it that much easier to show furniture to my design clients. I could simply walk them from the studio into the showroom to test the pieces as we talked about fabrics and other custom details.

Jamie, Krista, and I planned a two-week vacation to the Bahamas for that July. I had scheduled my annual mammogram for the week before we were leaving. As is the case for many women, I got a call to come back in for a second test. But then, the day after that second mammogram, I got another call, directly from my doctor, saying that we needed to schedule a biopsy and that his nurse would be in touch soon to get my appointment on the calendar.

I was a bit dumbstruck when the doctor called, but when the nurse followed up with me only minutes later, I'd regained my wits.

"I'm sorry, but I'm leaving on vacation."

"Debbe, you need to come in immediately."

"It's two weeks in the Bahamas."

We scheduled the biopsy for right after I returned from our holiday.

The day after the biopsy, I found out I had cancer. Jamie called to see if I'd heard from the doctor just as my call with the doctor ended.

"Have you heard anything?"

"Yeah, I just got off the phone."

"And?"

"Yeah. I have breast cancer."

"I'm coming home now."

"You really don't have to. It's going to be fine."

"I'm coming home now."

Jamie went with me to the surgery consultation. As we checked in, I noticed a big display of breast cancer awareness paraphernalia for sale—T-shirts, hats, car decals, the works.

I thought to myself, *Ugh. I don't want any of that stuff. I'm not putting that sticker on my car. I don't wear baseball caps. And I'm not ever wearing pink!*

That night, in bed, Jamie was a mess—tearing up as he shared his worries.

"Jamie, listen. It's going to be fine. We're going to be fine. I researched the surgeon. She's got a lot of experience with this."

I wasn't just saying that to console Jamie. I really did approach the whole event of my cancer with a bit of detachment. We simply needed to identify what had to be done and then get to doing it. Get surgery. Maybe do chemo or radiation. And that would be that.

Jamie brought me to the hospital early the morning of my surgery. Who else had shown up? My whole big fat Greek family. So far as I was concerned, that couldn't have been more horrible. Why were they making such a big fuss?

The doctor came to talk with me after the surgery was over.

"We didn't get it all."

"Are you kidding me?"

My cancer was in a weird spot, complicated by its closeness to lymph nodes.

Of course, I had to heal from the first surgery before there could be a second. There was one night in that process where I woke up with a hematoma—essentially a breast full of blood. I passed out in the bathroom, and so we had to go back to the doctor to take care of that.

I made sure no one in my family knew about my second surgery. But somehow or other, my mother managed to show up then, too.

"Geez, Ma. We're just gonna take it out and that's it, okay?"

I ended up needing radiation—twice a week for six weeks.

I refused to take any time off, so I would drive from Portsmouth to Lowell, get irradiated, and then go to the shop to work or teach a class or meet with a client.

By the time we got to Thanksgiving, I was exhausted. I couldn't contribute. I just lay there on my parents' couch all day.

Back in the summer, just before I had the mammogram that had started the whole health scare, I'd gotten a call from the Boston Design Center inviting me to apply to their Designer on Call program. The center is a to-the-trade series of showrooms housing designer brands from all over the world. Hosting Designers on Call was a way that the center made its showrooms accessible to the public. Each year they vetted and selected a team of fifteen professional designers to offer design services to the public in conjunction with the brands housed in the center's showrooms.

I remember talking on the phone with Krista as I was completing the application paperwork. "I don't know if I want to do this, Krista. It's a significant commitment."

"Ma! If this opportunity had come your way a decade ago, you would have jumped at it!"

"I know. But it's happening now, not ten years ago."

"You'd better just apply."

I applied and got notice of acceptance around the Thanksgiving holiday. The program got started in December, just as I was finishing up my final weeks of radiation.

Early in January, we had our first "official" meeting as that year's group of affiliated designers. I was honored to have been accepted but also felt unsure of whether and how I might fit in. I don't say this often, but I was intimidated. Quite honestly, I didn't know what to expect. Some of the designers I met had been in that program for more than twenty years. Continuing on required making it through a review process, being invited to reapply, and then getting invited back as part of the on-call team for the next year. It was a serious business.

By the time of the January 2016 meeting, the Boston Design Center was under new ownership and new management. Management set a prerequisite that each of us designers needed to have a website of our own as well as be active on social media. Seven of the designers who had been at the center for some time didn't have either a website or a professional social media presence. They had their business cards, and word of mouth had been enough to sustain their careers.

On the day that we gathered to have professional headshots taken for the Boston Design Center website, I was standing in line ahead of one of my colleagues named Penny. I was already feeling like I'd been thrown to the wolves. No one at the center seemed particularly eager to help those of us who were new, not even the showroom representatives. I may have been running my own business, but I didn't know how things worked in this place, and Penny quickly became a mentor for me, helping me understand my role as an ambassador. She would stay on for another three years before retiring, though several of the others in that group of older designers would retire before her. For many of them, retirement came on the heels of observing that the design world was changing in ways they were uninterested in or unwilling to keep up with.

Being associated with the Boston Design Center turned out to be wonderful. There were cocktail parties and other fun events, including Boston Design Week, as well as lots and lots of education and training. I accumulated continuing education credits on topics from plumbing to ADA compliance, and once a month we attended a meeting at which we learned about all the new products available through the center.

During the period leading up to joining the Boston Design Center, I'd gotten invited to be a weekly guest on Jack Baldwin's *Jack's Café* show on WCAP 980 AM in Lowell. I'd done some redesign work for Jack and his girlfriend in their loft space. The couple needed to combine their styles when they moved in together, and Jack's girlfriend and I had worked carefully to make their shared space just right.

I'd not met Jack at any point in the redesign process, but he loved the result and reached out to me to see if I'd like to do a weekly segment on his show. That's how *Shabby Chic in Lowell with Debbe Daley* was born. In a sense, the show was an extension of my work for the *Lowell Sun* but in the form of a conversation about topics from antiquing to design to paint color selection.

Jack Baldwin, 980WCAP Radio, Chris Poublon, Gerry Lauderdale, and Debbe Daley.

I remember a Mother's Day segment that I did with Jack, during which I recounted a memorable holiday experience my sister Gina and I created for our mother. To make the day special, we'd planned a surprise picnic in the park. We were lucky that the weather was beautiful that afternoon, and so we'd been able to use furniture and tablecloths from our respective homes. Together, Gina and I set up an outdoor experience that made the picnic unique. The special event didn't require a lot of money, though it did require some planning and preparation. We set the prettiest tableau using vintage glassware, family linens, and holiday platters, and we even made sure that we served iced tea and lemonade using the glass bottles from the local dairy farm in Dracut—the very dairy that had delivered milk to us when we were kids.

We made pretty—and meaningful—everything about that afternoon. My mother appreciated it, and listeners to the show loved the recommendations for utilizing everyday pieces and family heirlooms as part of special events. Honestly, that's what my design style was all about: finding ways to enhance spaces—no matter where they were—with a combination of meaningful treasures and beautiful but useful objects.

Jack was fun and funny. The theme song for my segment was a bit from the Crosby, Stills, Nash & Young song "Our House." We put out a weekly show for three years before Jack had an accident that landed him in a rehab facility and took him away from his recording studio for quite some time.

During that same period, I was doing a tremendous amount of traveling back and forth between Portsmouth and Lowell. I did my very best to schedule appointments with clients in the order I'd pass them driving from home to work, or vice versa, so at least I wasn't eating up time backtracking along the route. I addressed all the different projects I had going on by being organized and strategic about the use of my time.

Everything was going well, until it wasn't.

I'd recently stopped being president of RESA New England, but I was still teaching at Middlesex and with ADE, and I was still active in IDS and ASID. I was writing for the *Huffington Post* and the *Lowell Sun*. I had the furniture store and design studio in Lowell. And I was active in the Philoptochos Society at my church—a women's philanthropic group with a full schedule of meetings, events, and fundraising activities.

I was overwhelmed, and I didn't appreciate feeling like I couldn't find time for my family or for enjoying my relationship with Jamie. I needed to step back and reassess my life choices, decide what was really important to me, and prioritize. I also needed to recognize that it was okay to pause for a bit, reset, and look to the future rather than simply be caught up in whatever I needed to achieve on a given day.

I let go of a couple of my professional society memberships. I kept writing for the *Lowell Sun*, but when Arianna left the *Huffington Post*, I took that as a sign to let go of that activity.

I maintained R.A.W. Furnishings for a while but eventually arrived at a point where it, too, felt like too much. Being responsible for the showroom and its employees, being present for festivals and events, or just ensuring that I was there to help unload furniture shipments from giant trailer trucks that weren't allowed to come down historic cobblestone streets and couldn't fit into narrow back alleys—the whole enterprise made me feel like I was under a lot of pressure. So, in 2018, we held a big sale at R.A.W. A dear friend, Cathy Coneeny, ended up buying a number of items to sell at the Canal Street Antique Mall in Lawrence. The rest of what was left we used to furnish a house that Krista had just purchased.

Letting go of some of these projects and responsibilities allowed me to focus on the design business and on family. It also helped keep my sanity intact. I stopped feeling scatterbrained and inefficient. I got to go skiing and snowboarding with Jamie, and I got to go to New York quite a bit to visit Krista when she still had her apartment there. She and I cooked Thanksgiving dinner together one year instead of spending the holiday with extended family. We watched the Macy's Thanksgiving Day Parade from her balcony, and we got to have a special day together, just the two of us.

To the extent that I also stepped away from social media during that time, I let go of what was becoming a major tool and resource for design professionals. I didn't connect back into the social media landscape until 2018. The catalyst for my reentry was an event called the Design Influencers Conference, which that year took place in Beverly Hills.

It was the best conference I'd ever attended. Everyone there was talking about blogging and being an influencer. I made fast friends with California designer Wendy Glaister. The two of us got talking about media opportunities, and I came to understand that I had access to more opportunities in the New England area than she did out in Modesto. I invited her to speak at the Boston Design Center. A little later on, and once Wendy established herself on the speaking circuit, she and I partnered to develop a continuing education course for the Interior Design Educators Council. That led to joint speaking opportunities, including at new venues for me like the San Francisco Design Center, Las Vegas Market, and Desert Design Days in Arizona.

Debbe Daley speaking at the Boston Design Center.

As my travel schedule increased and I got back into social media, I thought about one of the members of our Greek church who had stood out to me when I was a young girl. Everyone had to dress up for church, but some of the women always seemed to take that requirement to another level. They would dress to the nines. One of those women was an interior designer whose appearance and success I revered.

Later on, when I was in my late twenties and working several jobs, she came into the flooring store one evening while I was there and started up a conversation with the owner. She was dressed up then, too, fancy hat and all. I was sitting behind the desk, listening to her tell him what she needed—this rug, that tile, and on from there. I smiled and said hi to her when she looked my way.

The next day, I told my parents, "Oh my God, that designer from church came to the store last night while I was there!"

"Oh, she's married to a doctor, I think," my mom chimed in.

After I'd started writing for the *Lowell Sun*, my mother shared with me that this same woman I'd admired had been overheard by one of my mother's friends saying, "Can you believe Debbe Daley is writing interior design advice? She's not even an interior designer!"

That bit of gossip stung quite a bit. I learned that what disqualified me in this woman's eyes was that I hadn't received a four-year degree in design. For that reason, the title *interior designer* would never be more than a title I'd given myself—like a little girl playing house with her parents' china.

Later on, when I started at the Boston Design Center, I learned that this woman had been a card-carrying member for years. The center held a milestone anniversary bash early in my tenure there—a great big event, one with a lot more younger designers than older ones, including students from Boston Architectural College who were there to help work the event and make connections. The crowd was mingling, the music was booming, and people were dancing and generally enjoying themselves.

I saw the fancy designer walk in with her husband. As on that night when she'd come into the flooring store, once again I was sitting behind the main desk. They entered the room looking as sophisticated as ever.

That's when she looked over at me and promptly turned away.

But unlike that night in the flooring store, my attitude about her had changed. Then, I'd considered her a model to be emulated. Now, from my vantage point at the welcome desk, she and her husband didn't fit the scene. I assume they felt the same way, because they were gone within fifteen minutes. For a moment, I felt badly. I wished they could have embraced the crowd, found a way to relate to the designers who represented a new generation—even newer than me.

After about four years of watching so many of the older designers retire from the Boston Design Center or not be selected to return for another year, I decided to start a private Facebook group where trade professionals could share knowledge and information and keep one another abreast of trends—both in design and in business. I wanted to be sure that I continued learning and that what I saw happen to those aging designers at the center wouldn't also happen to me or to anyone coming up after me.

I didn't want older designers to become irrelevant, and I didn't want newer designers to have to reinvent the wheel. Most of all, I felt it was imperative to establish a group where sharing resources and business strategies was the norm. I didn't want other people to have the same experience I did back when I was trying to establish myself as a designer. I wanted to be sure that I helped create a space where new design professionals could find up-to-date information and tools to help move their careers forward and where a strong sense of community held sway.

I called the Facebook group Design for Today. About six months after establishing our little community, I decided to host a conference at the Sheraton on the seacoast near our home in Portsmouth. I had already started planning it when my colleague Marianne Cherico, who was a member of the Real Estate Staging Association chapter that I'd started in Massachusetts, invited me to lunch. She had just launched her own podcast and wanted to talk about having me on as one of her guests.

Marianne also invited Wendy Woloshchuk, another Massachusetts designer, to join us. I had heard Wendy's name but didn't otherwise know her before the three of us sat down together one afternoon.

Our interests overlapped so well that we ended up having a four-hour lunch. I told them about the Facebook group I'd started and the conference I was planning.

"Who's sponsoring your event?" Wendy asked.

"No one."

"Well, who's paying for it?"

"I'm gonna pay for it."

"Okay, well, what are you gonna charge people for attending?"

"I don't know. Maybe ninety-nine dollars?"

"What!" Both Wendy and Marianne were beside themselves. "With all your experience?"

They offered to lend their expertise to the event and help me plan it.

We shifted from lunch to cocktails as we got deeper into brainstorming and strategizing. The restaurant usually closed between lunch and dinner service, but they agreed to let us stay during the interim period.

I started thinking about the connections I could call on as event sponsors—Benjamin Moore, Hunter Douglass, the Boston Design Center. We talked about the variety of workshops we would present. In the end, twenty-five designers attended the event. All the different sponsors sent representatives to give presentations. Marianne, Wendy, and I spoke on a variety of topics. And we ended the day with a group dinner downtown at which everyone enjoyed themselves.

When people started asking for the dates of the next gathering, I realized we needed to change the name of the Facebook group from Design for Today to Design for Today Collaborative to acknowledge Marianne's and Wendy's contributions. In the three years after that first conference, the group grew to include over eight hundred members. Marianne, Wendy, and I each offer a live video per week, with Marianne often focusing on mindset coaching, Wendy on business processes, and me on design. The three of us have a lot of fun working together to make the group a safe forum for anyone to pose a question without feeling stupid or inadequate. And we share all the trade knowledge and information we have—the products and tools we utilize to make our businesses run and the ways we maximize those tools to our benefit. The goal of the group is to keep others, especially those new to the industry, from spinning their wheels, posting the same questions over and over across social media sites and never really getting a sufficient answer.

Administering that Facebook group is a very satisfying project for me. Through it, I get to work against the trend that dominated the industry through much of my career—the tendency for the luxury design community to be cliquish, to shun newcomers, to refuse to share knowledge with those not properly initiated. It feels so good to pay forward something better than what I experienced myself.

DESIGN FOR TODAY
COLLABORATIVE

Marianne Cherico   Debbe Daley   Wendy Woloshchuk

One of my favorite activities that we've added to the group's experience is touring the High Point Market together. It's thrilling to meet members from across the country, and it gives me great satisfaction to be able to share the knowledge that I've gained over the years of building a business on my own.

I know from personal experience that it's possible to home in on a career you love and find the right resources to help you along, even when you cut your own nontraditional path. And I'm glad that the "rules" have changed, that the American Society of Interior Designers and the Interior Design Society, along with some others, recognize years of practicing a craft—and not just a four-year degree—as a qualification for being counted a professional in the field.

The reason I encourage others to give what they're passionate about a try when it comes to generating income is that I've managed to do just that—even during a time when long-standing traditions

It's possible to home in on a career you love and find the right resources to help you along, even when you cut your own nontraditional path.

113

about what makes a qualified designer and what counts as luxury design were just starting to be challenged. I was sitting in that audience in the early 1980s when a room full of traditionally trained designers gasped at the suggestion that there would be a major shift within the profession away from a more formal aesthetic. And I was there at the Boston Design Center in the late twenty-teens when the woman who said that I was firmly *not* an interior designer found herself ill at ease in a room full of relaxed and talented young people dancing and celebrating everything that was new and different about the design world.

I'm living proof that a person can stick with their passions and find ways to support themselves by pursuing them. Of course, the thing never to forget is that being an entrepreneur is work. You have to do the work. Whether things are going poorly or going well, there's no coasting.

In the end, there's also no going it alone. Entrepreneurs need to be surrounded by like-minded people. Those are the people who energize you precisely by reminding you that you're not alone. They're the people who will push you forward, make sure you keep learning and stay engaged, and even sometimes become your teammates or your biggest cheerleaders.

A person can stick with their passions and find ways to support themselves by pursuing them. Of course ... you have to do the work. ... There's also no going it alone.

I got my start in interior design by keeping engaged with my passions and by deciding at a relatively young age to pursue my independence and keep trying for a happy life. It's been a struggle at various points along the way.

Life sometimes travels in directions we couldn't have anticipated.

And sometimes, other people come along and challenge even our firmest commitments.

I remember the day that Jamie challenged my firm belief that I would never marry again. We'd been together for a decade, and everything about our companionship had been wonderful—right up until the day he said to me, "Debbe, you're tough, and you're stubborn, and I know that you can take care of yourself. But I want you to let me take care of you."

"I can take care of myself, Jamie."

"Deb, I *want* to take care of you," he said, trying again, then paused and turned that declaration into a question. "Will you let me take care of you?"

Until Jamie, there was no relationship I'd been in about which I would have said, "This is the person I will be with for the rest of my life."

Why did he have to ask me to confirm it?

Chapter Eight

PIVOT

The little loft that I'd purchased in Lowell after Jamie encouraged me to buy something for myself is a space I now refer to as the teaching loft. I've spent several years renovating it—arranging various structural transformations as I've been able to afford them—and students in my private classes get to practice measuring the space to create design plans, as if they were outfitting a new build. The loft has large windows, columns, and a very open floor plan—which can be a challenge for students just learning how to place furniture. It's a great venue for meeting clients in the Lowell area, and if I need to, it's a place where I can stay overnight instead of having to drive back home to Portsmouth.

Lowell teaching loft.

Recently, I've found myself asking those big life questions again: Who am I now? Where am I going next? And what *else* do I love to do? The answers are still taking shape, even shifting shape. If I look at my own enjoyments, I find the thread that holds me together. That's how I continue to make sense of different interests that might seem outwardly like they're not part of the same trajectory. That's even true of my early work experience—from my business degree to the different jobs I held in a corporate environment. Later, these helped me be able to own and run a business.

Figuring out who I am and how I make a living by following my passions—that's been an ongoing project. There was no epiphany, no moment when all my efforts coalesced into a perfect outcome. There may have been some moments when I thought I knew exactly who I was and what I wanted next, but those weren't final or lasting. Even now, having established myself as an interior designer and built a life around that, there's still more to go, still more to be determined.

The point that I'm at right now is one that feels a bit uncomfortable, even scary. I've been rethinking how I present myself to the world—on my website, on social media, through the different organizations in which I'm an active member, through my teaching, and, of course, through my engagement with clients. I've also been sharing more of myself lately with a much bigger audience than I ever thought I would. For all my efforts to be independent and to do what feels right, there's always that voice in the back of my mind: *What are people going to think about me taking this step? Will they welcome me? Will my current inclination to focus on the little things I enjoy—like my vintage dishes and my gardening and my experiments in the kitchen— make people wonder what on earth I'm up to?*

I'm used to my family knowing a lot about me. Krista can predict my taste and sometimes even my very words. My father will say things like "One thing you've got to know about Debbe is to just let her go with whatever she decides to do. She's stubborn. She's going to make her own mistakes. She'll probably succeed. But just let her go and do it." Jamie will help me drag a giant piece of driftwood out of the river without asking, "Deb, what are we doing towing a whole tree trunk on top of the boat?" But letting people I don't know find out more about me than my design work? Scary.

I'm noticing that it helps, at this point in my development, to think about the path that brought me here—because at times, *that* path was scary and uncomfortable, too. But from my vantage point now, whatever discomforts there were appear totally worth it. Frankly, I would hesitate to consider the alternatives: What if I hadn't decided to leave my daughter's father and take a chance on creating happiness in my life and hers? What if I hadn't gotten trained in redesign, or organized free classes at the local library, or asked for opportunities to promote my work when I moved to Lowell?

My strong sense is that most of the activities that push us further along our paths are likely to be uncomfortable. Growth will always have its awkward moments. That's part of what makes it so easy for naysaying and negativity to hold us back.

There will always be plenty of people who don't respond positively. For that reason alone, moments of transition in careers and in life are precisely the times when, if it's at all possible, we need to gather our supporters and our biggest cheerleaders. We need to remember that when we share our true selves and share what we know, there *will* be people out there with whom that's going to resonate, people who will respond positively to what we're trying to create. I still have to tell myself, *Something about you is going to appeal to someone. That's why so many people in any given creative field have jobs.*

Moments of transition in careers and in life are precisely the times when … we need to gather our supports and our biggest cheerleaders.

The cheerleaders and people who already know us well might be the very people who help us see where along our paths we might travel next. Honestly, it's taken a number of people around me to encourage me to take this next step in my career. It's taken Jamie pointing out to me that I don't always notice how I put 200 percent effort into everything I do. It's taken friends and family noticing the unique community I'm creating online. It's taken my web designer, Michael, who has been with me for well over a decade, propelling me forward with candid insights like "Deb, I've been watching your career for a long time now. The reason you're wondering about whether all the different activities you're engaged in make a coherent whole is that it's not just about interior design anymore. It's about you. People aren't just engaging with your room designs; they like seeing you gardening, cooking, seeing what you're wearing, where you're traveling—the whole thing. You're writing, you're speaking, you're coaching and mentoring others; you've got a paint color and a furniture line—but all these things come together because they're all very much *you*."

I understood what he was saying, but it also seemed strange to me. My life is like everyone else's: I cut and arrange the hydrangeas that grow in my yard. I run into the T.J. Maxx to hunt for treasure while I'm waiting for the dog to be groomed. I still work hard at my job.

It's some combination of those cheerleaders and people who know me well plus an expanding sense of community that boosts my courage to move forward. I've met wonderful designers from all over the world and some that have become true friends of mine—a group of girlfriends who freely share business dilemmas, give one another advice, and bond over personal matters.

I'm involved in organizations that reflect my design aesthetic and my mission for my business. People I don't know recognize my brand with comments like "I knew that was your design!" or "That's so you!" Other forms of recognition in the field—like being selected for brand ambassadorships, guest spots on industry shows, or exclusive design groups, or being asked to provide coaching services at industry-wide conferences—I take these as signs that it's time to pivot to something new.

One of the best aspects of this moment is bonding with people who have also decided to take their lives in a new direction. A connection of mine recently pivoted from being a lawyer to being a landscape architect. Some of my students are shifting from careers they hated or have grown bored with to careers they're excited about. Even Krista, who spent twelve years in the fashion industry in New York City, decided recently to train for an entirely different career. She's in law school as I write this.

Krista's LIM College Graduation

For each of us, our real drivers are the activities that tap into our creativity. I think that's true even for people in fields that aren't considered to be "creative." Often the things we enjoy doing turn out to be those that allow us to feel like we are making something meaningful. To the extent that we can embrace those things, we're likely to increase our chances at happiness.

Just like me, your path is yours alone. It's personal. The idea is to find and stay true to yourself at each step along the way. Being true to yourself means recognizing that you can start over, but not at your own expense. Whatever you choose has to seem right for you. You're good at certain things. You

For each of us, our real drivers are the activities that tap into our creativity.

enjoy certain things that you're good at. Turning those into a means of making a living requires both putting yourself out there and finding a community of like-minded people. Professional groups, opportunities for learning something new or something more—these can be sources of support and encouragement. And because your path is yours alone, you can always pivot as you create a life that you can be happy with.

My approach is still what it's always been. I want to be happy. I want my family to be happy. I want Krista to be true to herself and happy with her life. And I want to know that I did everything possible to support myself and my daughter by making a career doing what I love.

I've held on to my independence by having my own place, my own car, my own business. And when I met Jamie, I was committed to never being married again. He didn't want to be married either.

Until one day when he did.

That was the day he told me he wanted to take care of me. "I'm serious," he said. "Deb, I want you and me and Krista to be a family."

Hearing him say that made me nervous. In a way, we'd already happily become members of one another's families. We'd made a home together. We'd figured out how to be independent people who love spending time with one another.

I went out to the driveway to sit in my car. I leaned on the steering wheel and called my brother.

"Nick, what is going on?" I asked, just before I started crying uncontrollably. "I don't want to mix my things with Jamie's things. What if it doesn't work out?"

"Deb. He wants to take care of you. Did you ever have that?" Nick followed up with "Do you have any doubts about him?"

I hadn't doubted him. There had never been any red flags with Jamie. None.

"Then, just go with it!"

Eventually, I went back in the house. "Okay, fine." I said to Jamie. "We will try it."

"No, Deb. We are not trying this. I know you don't need me to take care of you. But I want you to be my wife, and we are not just going to try it out."

I'd never met anyone like Jamie, nor had I been part of any partnership that felt so right.

For the wedding, we planned a little reception, just thirty people, all of them our closest family members. I did not want to acquire a new wedding dress—I had been there and done that—but I wanted to wear something meaningful to me, to us.

I've always been a fan of toile patterns, which tend to have romantic, pastoral scenes or vignettes printed in a single color on a light background. Toile tells a story—about travel, about family, about lifestyle. On one of my business trips to Paris, a group of us designers had visited the Pierre Frey showroom during Paris Design Week. I love both the products and the history of that design house—the passing along of craft and art through generations of a single family—and I'd loved a particular toile fabric that we saw on our visit. It had an ivory background with characters in grayish outline, tinged with a bit of yellow.

After returning home, and at the Pierre Frey showroom in Boston, I'd seen a full wing of that same fabric and ordered three yards right on the spot. This was the fabric from which I would sew my wedding dress. All its vignettes spoke to our story: people making music together, hiking, gardening, fishing, going on adventures. There was a little bit of everything that comprised our family. I'd learned to sew without using patterns, but I purchased and used two as guides to make a tea-length, A-line, halter-top dress—something I would happily wear again for another special occasion. Two days before the wedding, I started putting it all together.

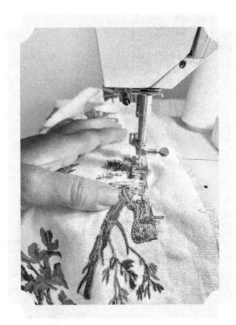

Sewing of the wedding dress.

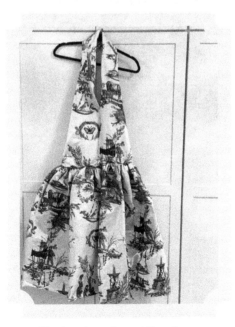

The hand-made wedding dress.

Wedding reception in hydrangea alley at our Cedar Bungalow.

Dad, me, and Mom walking down the aisle.

The Greek wedding crown ritual ceremony: Jamie, Debbe, and Krista with Brad Byrd.

We had a Greek ceremony in the local Greek church; we even followed the Greek tradition of wearing our wedding bands on our right hands instead of the left. For the reception, we hosted a New England–style lobster bake in our front yard. It rained all week long, but it was bright and sunny on the day itself. We used white and blue hydrangeas from the garden as decoration, played music on the Sonos, and had a perfect day together with everyone enjoying one another's company.

Jamie and Debbe, wedding reception in hydrangea alley.

My family's experiences—my grandparents and parents in particular—have shaped the person I am today, the things I do, and the people I love. I started sewing in the basement of my parents' house on the machine my grandparents purchased for me at a yard sale. My fashion sense developed from my mother's ability to mix and match the clothes we had available to us as kids. My penchant for antiquing follows my grandfather's footsteps. And my desire to act with integrity comes from both my parents, my father especially.

In a phone call about a month ago, my father reminded me that he hadn't seen me in a few weeks.

"I know you're busy, Deb. Where are you flying off to now?"

"I'm headed to Napa, Dad."

"Oh! It's beautiful out there." He paused. "That's going to be expensive."

"Dad, it's an all-expenses-paid trip."

"Really?"

"It is."

"How's the new build at the beach coming along?"

"It's almost done. And then I'm heading down to High Point for the spring market."

"Deb …" His voice took on a tone I wasn't used to hearing. "Are you having fun?"

I couldn't believe my ears.

I smiled. "Yeah, I am having fun."

"You know what, Deb? That's really all that matters, isn't it? That you're having fun doing what you're doing."

Dad and me on our front beach of our home we call "The Cedar Bungalow."

9 781642 256499